THE BEST BOOK OF URBAN MYTHS EVER!

This is a Carlton book

This edition published 1998 by Carlton Books Limited,
20 St Anne's Court, Wardour Street, London W1V 3AW

ISBN 1 85868 559 1

Printed and bound in Great Britain

THE BEST BOOK OF URBAN MYTHS EVER!

Yorick Brown and Mike Flynn

CARLTON

CONTENTS

ACCIDENTS

Accidents are, by their very nature, random events. There is nothing funny about someone being hurt as the result of an attack, but there is something rather hilarious about the cruel hand of fate wrecking someone's dignity in a random accident.

Perhaps the only thing funnier is the accident that occurs as a result of gross stupidity. This is the kind of accident that you can see coming from a mile off, but is somehow all the funnier for that. Any story that mentions a secret smoker, a leaky fuel pipe and a fireworks factory in the opening sentence is really telling you everything you need to know. We can all fill in what happens from there, but we still laugh at the conclusion.

There is also the slapstick element - when, in a film, two men attempt to walk across a street carrying a huge sheet of glass the audience knows that they are never going to make it to the other side. It is one of the great clichés of the cinema, but it is still funny, even after all this time.

The tales that follow are about people who ignored all of the warning signs. Read them and perhaps you'll think twice about walking fearlessly under a ladder, on the grounds that you refuse to be thought of as superstitious.

THE ULTIMATE DUMP?

It could happen to anybody. A couple came home one evening to discover a huge gaping hole in the roof, their dog dead and their furniture soaked in gallons of foul-smelling matter. Distressed and baffled by what they saw, they called the police who duly arrived to investigate. After several phone calls, the detective was finally able to ascertain what had happened. It seemed that the container holding the waste from the lavatories on a passing Boeing 737 had burst open. The contents froze in the atmosphere as they fell toward the ground, and the resulting block of ice had smashed through the roof of the unlucky couple's house, killing their dog before melting all over their belongings.

RAIN MAN

Firefighters in New Zealand were puzzled to find the charred body of a man amongst the debris of a recent forest fire. Quite why he was wearing a full scuba-diving outfit in the middle of a forest fire some 30 miles inland was far from clear... Once the man was identified and it was determined where he had been diving, it didn't take long for investigators to come up with the answer. Firefighters had used helicopters equipped with huge scoops to collect water from the Tasman sea 32 miles away, which they dumped from a safe height on to the raging inferno. A very unlucky scuba-diver, happily gazing at schools of fish, must have been quite surprised to be suddenly scooped from the depths, taken to the heavens and then released - only to plummet to a fiery death.

STICKY PROBLEM

It's hard not to sympathize with the man from Newcastle, England who returned home and went straight to toilet after an evening of drunken merriment rounded off by a visit to an Indian restaurant. As a regular sufferer from hemorrhoids, the man assigned the pangs of pain in his backside to his familiar problem rather than the hot curry he had just eaten. Somewhat embarrassed by this recurring ailment, he had previously hidden the hemorrhoids cream in a cupboard below the bathroom sink and so as usual, he took out the tube and smeared the contents over the affected area. To his dismay, he realized that instead of relief, he found himself unable to withdraw his hand from between his buttocks. It was then that he took a look at the tube he had taken from the cupboard only to discover that he'd grabbed a tube of super-fast glue instead of hemorrhoids cream. As a result, he had firmly stuck his buttocks together with his hand in-between for good measure.

DEALING WITH IN-LAWS

Stag parties can be risky, but this experience would make any husband-to-be have second thoughts about holding a last bachelor celebration. At a ski resort in Austria, the stag party was in full, drunken swing when the participants took to the slopes for some night-time skiing. The so-called friends of the husband-to-be proceeded to tie him, naked, to a sledge and send him flying down the slope. Unbeknown to them, the bride-to-be's father was enjoying a relaxing stroll at the bottom of the same slope. Powerless to do anything other than shout "Get out of the way!", the naked sledger failed to attract the attention of the man who was soon to become his father-in-law. Instead, the sledge rammed into the man, killing him instantly. The wedding was replaced by a funeral – and the marriage was, unsurprisingly, called off.

WRONG KIND OF PUSSY

A woman came home one day to find her boyfriend lying naked and unconscious, face-down under the sink in the bathroom. Looking him over, she felt a small bump on his head and also found some mysterious scratches around his groin. While she was wondering whether she should call an ambulance, her boyfriend recovered and was able to explain what happened. He had been about to take a shower when he dropped a new bar of soap under the sink. Bending down to retrieve it, he suddenly felt intense pain around his groin, which startled him so much that he hit his head on the sink and knocked himself out. Examining the scratches, they both agreed that they looked like they could have been made by a cat – which puzzled them both, because they didn't own one. A little later they found that their neighbours' kitten was in their flat and worked out that the kitten must have sneaked into the bathroom. When the boyfriend was bending under the sink, the kitten presumably regarded his dangling genitals as an interesting toy, and swiped at them with claws fully extended.

DON'T TOUCH THIS

A few years ago a plane flying across the Gulf of Mexico crashed, killing all 82 passengers. Investigators were mystified as to the cause of the accident – it had passed a thorough inspection before take-off, the pilots had not reported any problems and there had been no distress calls. Further investigations revealed nothing and rumours about the plane being another casualty of the Bermuda Triangle propagated. Some months later, however, the plane's black box was discovered washed up on a Mexican beach. Investigators listened to the recordings and hear the last words that the pilot spoke: "I wonder what happens when I press this button." They have still to find out which button the pilot pressed.

TRIPLE TRAGEDY

This tragic story makes everyone weep. A nanny was working for a family with three children – a pair of three-year-old twin girls and a six-month-old baby boy. One day, she was giving one of the twins a bath while the other girl was in the next room looking after the baby. The little girl was holding the baby in her arms and spinning around when she slipped and banged his head on the corner of a cupboard. When the girl saw blood coming from the back of the baby's head, she was so frightened she ran out of the room, out of the house and into the street only to be run over by a speeding car. The nanny, hearing the squeal of brakes outside, went out to see what was going on and was hysterical when she found out that the girl was dead. A neighbour tried to comfort the nanny, but when she took her back inside, she discovered that the other twin, left unattended in the bath, had drowned. A few minutes later, the neighbour also discovered the baby had died from the head injury.

INNOCENT FUN

A young female hairdresser was just about to close up shop when a man came in and requested a haircut. The man had all the appearance of a dirty old man including the long coat, and the woman was a little uneasy about being alone with him in the shop. Confident, however, that she could look after herself, the hairdresser agreed to give him a quick cut and told him to sit down. Winking, the man gave her a slimy smile as she wrapped a sheet around him. When she turned back from picking up her scissors and comb, she noticed that the man was performing a rhythmic up-and-down motion under the sheet. Presuming that the dirty old man was masturbating, the hairdresser grabbed a nearby vase and cracked him over the head with it before calling the police. When the police arrived, they removed the sheet only to discover that all the poor man had been doing was cleaning his glasses. Naturally, the aggrieved customer later pressed charges against the hairdresser for assault and battery.

RUSTY STAPLED NUTS

A man who worked in a machine shop found a preference for masturbating to the whirring noises of the machinery he tended, when no one was around. Unfortunately, during one such escapade, he slipped and caught his scrotum in the drive belt. Although he tore his scrotum and lost a testicle, being rather innovative he bravely stapled his scrotum back together and carried on working. A week later, however, he was forced to see a doctor and explain the cause of his injury because the staples began to rust.

BUTTHOLE BUSKER

A man who lost his house keys was so desperate to get into his home that he tried to crawl in through the cat flap. Of course, he underestimated his size and became wedged in the flap, unable to go further in or back out. He tried shouting for help only to attract the attention of some mischievous youths who spotted this as an opportunity to have some fun. They pulled down the poor man's trousers and then painted a face on his behind, stuck a flower between his buttocks and placed a sign declaring it a work of art. Despite his pleas, he remained stuck there for three days whilst passers-by admired his derriere and threw coins between his legs. Although the man's pride was severely dented, the stunt earned him £200.

WATER HAZARD

A golfing fanatic was so furious after playing a losing shot that he threw his bag of clubs into a nearby lake and stomped off. Other golfers weren't at all surprised, however, when five minutes later, he returned red-faced, took off his shoes, rolled up his trousers and waded into the lake. Noone was too surprised at these second thoughts – it was clearly an expensive set of clubs he'd hurled into the water. After fumbling around for a while the bedraggled golfer fished out the golf bag, but to the amazement of the bystanders, he merely unzipped a pocket, took out a set of car keys, flung the set of clubs back into the water and stormed off again.

WHALE OF A TIME

Despite the big advance in technology in recent decades, laughable mistakes can still be made. For several months, the Swedish Navy had been convinced that foreign submarines were operating in Swedish waters. Despite a strongly-worded speech by the Foreign Minister at a United Nations conference, no government would admit to using submarines in Swedish territorial seas. Incensed, the Vice-Admiral decided enough was enough and launched a massive naval operation to uncover the offenders. After weeks of extensive searching filled with long days spent tracking sound waves around the Baltic Sea, it was concluded that the culprits were not submarines but a school of whales that had taken a liking to the area. Even so, the Vice-Admiral is still convinced that foreign vessels had been violating Swedish waters.

SUCK JOB

A salesman staying in San Diego returned to his motel a little tipsy after a few drinks in a local bar. Although it was about 12:30am, he decided to have a quick dip in the pool before retiring for the night. As noone was around, he didn't bother about getting his swimming shorts from his room – just stripped off and dived in. Around 2am, the motel caretaker was roused from a deep sleep by shouts coming from the pool area. He got dressed and wandered down to investigate what sounded like desperate pleas for help. In the pool, the salesman appeared to be struggling against the wall of the swimming pool. The clerk discovered that the man's penis had become stuck in the inlet to the pump that circulated water through the pool's cleaning and filtration plant. Without daring to ask how the swimmer got himself into this predicament, the caretaker switched off the power to the pump, but the man's penis had become so swollen that he still couldn't free himself. Paramedics were summoned and after careful consideration they applied lubrication around the entry to the pump. The very distressed salesman whose quick swim had turned into a very painful four-hour soak was eventually released with no long-term after effects.

DOUBLE TROUBLE

One summer's day, a couple had a few friends round for a barbecue. After everybody had eaten, the man of the house, who had been drinking since that morning, slipped on a piece of dropped meat and twisted his ankle badly. A friend immediately took the injured host to hospital. Meanwhile, the party came to an end, the guests left and the wife started cleaning up the mess. She noticed that the can of petrol her husband had been using to light the barbecue was virtually empty and, not wanting to contaminate the sink, she poured the contents down the outside toilet. A few minutes later, the husband returned from the hospital and his wife fussed over him before returning to finish the cleaning up. The husband had a need for the toilet, but because of his ankle couldn't make it upstairs so he went to the outside one. As he sat down, he lit himself a cigarette. By the time he noticed the smell of petrol, it was too late ...the toilet exploded.

HOT DISH

A man in San Diego bought a satellite dish and being rather miserly, he decided to set it up himself. Clambering up his ladder, he attached the dish to the side of his house. Then, with his wife inside shouting to him when the reception was best, he adjusted it. Finally satisfied, he and his wife relaxed for the night in front of the television. The next day was a real scorcher, but still enamoured by the satellite television on offer, the couple stayed in. That afternoon, they heard sirens and lots of shouting outside. The man went outside to find out the cause of the commotion and saw the house across the road on fire. The fire was put out, but the house was completely gutted, and the firemen couldn't work out how the fire had started. The man thought no more of it. The next day, however, a fire inspector was examining the charred remains when a sudden flash of sunlight caught his attention. The inspector eventually worked out that the neighbour's satellite dish had been concentrating the sun's rays on the curtains of the house and had caused the fire. The man was fined $2,000 and forced to take down his satellite dish. The next year he got cable.

UPHILL ALL THE WAY

A man was driving round the hilly streets of San Francisco on the way to a job interview, but he had got hopelessly lost and was already quite late. Passing a telephone box, he stopped the car and telephoned the company he had the interview with. As he was explaining his predicament to the secretary, he realized he'd forgotten to put his handbrake on and was shocked to see his car rolling down the hill towards him. Before he could do anything, the car had rammed into the telephone box, jamming him inside. Hearing him cursing, the sensitive secretary must have taken it personally and slammed the phone down on him. He waved to passers-by, but they just waved back. It wasn't until an hour later that it occurred to him to use the phone to contact the emergency services which promptly rescued him. Afterwards the man developed a sudden loathing for hills and left San Francisco for the much flatter San Diego.

WAITING PATIENTLY

An old couple had been together for over 60 years and their lives were deeply entwined. One day, the man dropped his wife off to do some shopping and told her he'd wait in the car for her. He turned on the radio and entertained himself with a bit of people-watching. Meanwhile, his wife had done her shopping and, completely forgetting about her husband, she walked home. When her husband didn't show up that evening, the wife got worried and reported him missing. He was found two days later exactly where she'd left him after a policeman noticed him asleep at the wheel.

THE SHORTCUT

A man was walking home from a long night at his local pub, and drunkenly decided to take a shortcut down a side street. He soon came to a fork in the street but couldn't remember which way would take him home so, he decided to take the left fork. Half an hour later he found he was lost. Feeling dizzy, he decided to rest a while and sat, then lay down on the pavement. His back soon ached, however, and he noticed it was softer further on, so he staggered up and lay down on the softer part of the pavement. A few hours later, he woke up and discovered he couldn't move. He looked around and realised that he was lying in a patch of cement - the cement had set while he slept. He spent the night unable to move and too embarrassed to shout for help. In the morning, eight hours later, the workmen came and chiselled him out. He was lucky it wasn't the weekend.

OVER THE TOP

Three school children, caught cutting class by their teacher, were given a whole term's detention for their misdemeanour. Thinking the punishment over the top, the kids decided to exact revenge on the teacher, sneaked into the teacher's staff room and emptied a packet of laxative into a coffee jar. Later that afternoon, half of the school's teachers were taken to hospital with severe abdominal pains. It seems that the children had misread the instructions on the box and given the teachers 100 times the recommended quantity.

SAUSAGES!

One summer weekend, a group of rugby-loving students at Southampton University decided to celebrate a victory by having a barbecue. There was plenty to drink and, in no time, the students were singing and vomiting all over the place. One student, particularly worse for wear, was feeling a bit hungry and he decided to put some more sausages on the barbecue. However, his wires must have got crossed somewhere along the line and, instead of opening a pack of sausages, he pulled out his penis and laid it on the barbecue. Five minutes later, he was found turning it this way and that with a spatula, seemingly oblivious to the pain, and was whisked off to casualty.

SMALL TALENT

A Russian man had an unusual talent for extremely small writing and would copy pages of writing on to minuscule pieces of paper. Seeking the biggest challenge for his talent, he decided to try to copy the entire works of Lenin on to a postage stamp. Every evening, he spent hours in his study copying pages on to a tiny section of the stamp. This went on for month after month until, 15 months, two weeks and four days later, he finally finished. He shouted for joy and went out to celebrate at his local bar. The next morning, the man, suffering a stinking hangover, went to his study to frame his accomplishment, but couldn't find the stamp anywhere. Having searched and searched unsuccessfully he asked his wife if she'd seen the stamp. "Stamp?" replied the woman nonchalantly, "Oh, yes, I needed one for a letter to my mother and found one on your desk yesterday. You didn't need it, did you?"

HOLLYWOOD STREAKER

Sleepwalking can be an embarrassing experience for anyone, but particularly for a middle-aged man from Los Angeles. On several occasions, the man had woken up to find himself walking down the street or climbing up a tree in his garden. In an effort to put a stop to these nightly jaunts he tried tying himself to his bedpost, but discovered he was quite an expert at untying knots whilst asleep. Events came to a head, when the man awoke to find himself strolling down Sunset Boulevard totally naked with hundreds of tourists gaping at him. Red-faced, the man grabbed a newspaper off a passer-by and ran into some public toilets where he hid for a few hours, only to be arrested for soliciting by an insensitive LA cop. He finally conquered his sleepwalking by handcuffing himself to his bedpost and giving his neighbour the key.

SAVE OUR SOULS

American viewers, responding to a new evangelical television programme, received a shock when they tried to make a phone donation. The evangelist in question had requested money to help him embark on a crusade to save lost souls. However, when people phoned the number he gave, they heard a woman panting and talking in seductive tones about all kinds of sexual practices. Apparently the evangelist had mistakenly reversed two digits of the phone number and inadvertently given the number for an X-rated sex chatline.

HIT AND RUN

A Somerset woman was driving home when suddenly a little girl ran out in front of her car. The woman slammed on her brakes, but it was too late and she hit the girl. Petrified, the woman drove off and when she got home, packed her bags and moved to London. After a year, the woman had settled in London, but wracked with guilt and missing her friends and family, she turned herself in. However, the police found no reports of a hit and run incident involving a little girl on that day. However, they did report that a pig had been run over. It seems that the pig had escaped a cider festival where it had been dressed up in a dress and bonnet.

THE SPICE OF LIFE

An Italian family received an unexpected package from an aunt who had emigrated to the USA some years before. On discovering that the package contained a jar of dark powder, the mother decided that it must be some exotic spice and, that evening, concocted a pasta sauce using the powder. The family were more than pleased with the strong meaty flavour the powder gave to their pasta dishes. However, they were more than distraught the next morning when they received a letter from their aunt telling them to expect their uncle's cremated remains any day.

BUN IN THE OVEN

This urban myth is more likely a scare story, but it has to be told. A couple from San Francisco asked the girl next door if she could babysit on Friday night so that they could go to the cinema. The girl readily agreed and, come Friday night, the couple left their baby with the girl. The couple enjoyed the film and decided to go for a drink before returning home, but the wife, like most mothers, was a little worried about her baby and decided to call to see if everything was all right. The phone was eventually answered by the girl, who told the mother everything was fine and that she had put the chicken in the oven for dinner. Satisfied, the mother joined her husband at the bar. As the mother recounted the conversation to her husband, it suddenly occurred to her that the girl had mentioned something about a chicken. Concerned, the couple returned home to find the girl freaking out. It seems the girl had taken LSD, and in her hallucination, taken the baby for a chicken and put it in the oven.

EMERGENCY CALL

A French man had just moved into an apartment on the outskirts of Paris. The phone hadn't been connected yet, so he went to a telephone box around the corner to phone his girlfriend and invite her round to his new flat. As he was chatting to his girlfriend, a man, looking as if he'd been sleeping on the streets for years, started banging on the telephone box. The man turned his back, ignored the tramp and continued talking to his girlfriend. Finally, the tramp screamed that it was an emergency and continued banging until the man relented, finished the conversation and hung up. Before he could admonish him, the tramp pushed past to use the phone. The man shrugged and returned to his apartment, but on turning the corner, realised why the tramp was making such a fuss – his apartment was on fire!

MISTAKEN IDENTITY

An American woman finally decided to visit her cousin, who had been put into a psychiatric institution, after putting it off for months. It was a cold day, so the woman took her winter coat, hat and gloves, and drove the 45 miles to the institution. On arriving, the reception was deserted, so the woman wandered around the corridors. Eventually she came across a nurse. When she asked the nurse where she could find her cousin, the nurse said, "Haven't you heard? Your cousin passed away last week. Oh, my dear, you must be devastated. Why don't you sit in here and I'll get you a cup of tea." The nurse took her into an empty room and took her coat, hat and gloves and told her she'd be right back. However, after waiting for nearly an hour, the woman went to see what happened. Suddenly, the woman was grabbed by two burly men and put into a strait jacket. The woman protested, "I'm not mad. I work in a bookshop!", but the psychiatrist just shrugged his shoulders and said, "That's what they all say." The woman's ID and money had been in her coat and her protests just confirmed to the psychiatrist that she was a raving lunatic. The woman was locked up for five years before finally proving her identity. The patient, who posed as a nurse, was never found.

DEAD BAGGAGE

Two sisters from Austin, Texas, took their elderly father for a holiday in the south of Mexico. A few days into their trip, however, the father had a heart attack and died. Distraught and possibly not thinking straight, the two sisters decide to try to take the body back themselves on the train, so that he could be buried in Texas. They propped their father up in their compartment to make it look like he was just sleeping. After a few hours, the train stopped for an hour at a small town, so the sisters got off to get something to eat and freshen up. They left their dead father on the train wrapped in a blanket, confident that no-one would touch him. The sisters spent so long looking for a place to eat that they lost track of time and had to run to catch the train. Panting, they finally returned to their compartment, but were shocked to discover that not only had a couple of drunken men taken over their compartment, but their father was nowhere to be seen. One sister, deciding to be blunt, told the men about their dead father. The drunken man turned to his companion and, laughing, said, "He was already dead. Thank goodness for that. My friend is so drunk, he dropped his suitcase on him and thought he killed him, so he threw him out the window a few miles back!"

ROCK LEGENDS

Most people know about the rock star's propensity to trash hotel rooms, but not many people know why. This story might explain their behaviour. A famous rock star, who shall remain nameless, was resting up in his hotel room in LA after an exhausting world tour. All he wanted that night was some well-deserved rest and peace and quiet, so after a long hot bath, the musician got into bed and attempted to get some sleep. However, his attempts at sleep were disturbed by a frantic buzzing sound. Realising it was a fly, he rolled up a magazine and tried to swat it, but the tired man kept missing. Getting increasingly frustrated, he kept going after the fly, ignoring the fact that he was knocking over furniture and breaking ornaments. At one point, he lost his footing and, hitting his head, knocked himself out. The musician was revived an hour later by angry hotel staff, who assumed the rock star had got drunk and wrecked his room. In pursuit of the elusive fly, he had caused over three thousand dollars' worth of damage and was banned from that particular hotel. He now takes a pet spider everywhere he goes.

THE GIANT RABBIT

A Frenchman was late for a fancy dress competition, so he took a shortcut across some fields. The only thing was that the man had dressed up as a rabbit, complete with floppy ears, and, unbeknown to him, the fields were popular for weekend hunters. One such hunter was astounded to see a giant rabbit hobbling on the other side of the field from him and, thinking it would feed his family for a year, took a pot shot at it. The hunter was even more astounded when he saw the rabbit jump up and start charging towards him, cursing loudly. After a somewhat bizarre confrontation, the man dressed as a rabbit and the hunter teamed up and won first prize in the fancy dress competition.

CHAIN REACTION

This story might serve as a warning to all litter bugs out there. An Italian woman was scoffing hazelnuts on a bus, when she came across a rotten one and promptly threw it out of a window. The driver of the car behind, unsure what it was, swerved out of the way. This caused another car to swerve, which in turn forced a five-ton truck to smash into a petrol station. The petrol station went up in flames and exploded everywhere. In all, 105 people were injured, 30 cars were written off and five shops and the petrol station were destroyed. An official, commenting on the incident, said "Thank God it wasn't a Brazil nut or the whole city might have gone up in flames!"

TOILET HOLIDAY

An old lady went for a week's holiday in the Lake District. Arriving at the hotel on Lake Windemere, she came across a toilet brush on the floor and picked it up to hand to the receptionist. Before she could say anything, the receptionist told her to clean the toilets on each floor. The old lady tried to explain who she was, but the receptionist was most insistent and the old lady didn't like to say no. With two sets on each of the five floors and, being a perfectionist, it took the old lady a good three hours to scrub down all the toilets. With the job done, she returned to the reception only to be reprimanded for taking so long and told to tidy up the rooms on the top floor. It was only when the old lady asked if she could see her room first and unpack her bags that the receptionist realised she was actually a paying guest and not the new chambermaid.

BEAR BELL

In Warsaw, Poland, a man went to a fancy dress party as a bear and proceeded to drink like a bear, downing one vodka shot after another. The drunken bear was eventually making such a commotion that the other party goers kicked him out. Feeling sad and dejected, the man stumbled home. However, on passing the local church, the man had an idea to rouse the boring residents of his home town. He broke into the church and entered the bell tower where he pulled the bell rope as hard as he could. However, instead of making the loud ringing sound he had hoped to, the man ended up 20 feet in the air and tangled in the ropes. Restricted by his bear suit he was unable to break free and remained hanging in the bell tower until a somewhat mystified priest found him two days later.

TRAGIC OUTCOME

This is one of those classic multiple-tragedy urban myths. The wife of a soldier, who was on a peace mission in Bosnia, was bathing her two children when the doorbell rang. As she rushed downstairs to answer the door, she tripped, fell and fatally knocked herself out. If she had been able to answer the door, she would've been told by a military officer that her husband had been killed by a sniper in Bosnia. To cement the tragedy, the two infants were found drowned in the bath.

FROM BAD TO WORSE

A rich American man was picked up by his chauffeur at the airport after a long business trip. The man asks his chauffeur what has been happening in his absence. "Well, sir, I'm afraid Rolly the dog died after he ate some burnt horseflesh. The stables burnt down after your mansion was consumed by fire." "Fire?" exclaimed the man. "Yes, sir," replied the chauffeur hesitantly, "The fire was caused from candles around the coffin of your dear mother, who died of a heart attack when she found out her husband, your stepfather, had run off with your wife." Uncomfortable with the silence that followed, the chauffeur added, "Apart from that, no news I can think of."

MISTAKEN IDENTITY

In Brussels, Belgium, a woman was on the bus when she thought she recognised a man sitting a few seats in front of her. "Hello, Frank," she called, but the man didn't turn around. She calls out several more times, but the man still failed to turn around. Finally, with everybody else on the bus looking at her, she went over and tapped the man on the shoulder. "Frank," she began, but stopped when the man turned around. Realising that she didn't know the man after all, she said, "Sorry, I thought you were the man I lost my virginity to," and, red-faced, she got off the bus.

A TAN TOO FAR

A woman living in Chicago was invited to her high school ten-year reunion in San Diego. The woman had once been the high school beauty queen, but the ten years that followed had not been kind to her. So, in a bid to spruce up her image, she decided to have an intense course of tanning treatments. She visited a tanning salon several times a day for the next week and by the end of it was glowing like the beauty she once was. Filled with the confidence the tan had given her, the woman boarded her flight to San Diego. Half an hour into the flight, however, the woman suddenly became aware of people sniffing around her and changing their seats away from her. Concerned, she asked the air hostess if there was a problem. Politely as she could, the air hostess informed her that the other passengers had complained of a burnt smell in her row. As soon as the flight arrived in San Diego, the woman checked into a hospital and the doctor confirmed her worst fears - she had cooked her insides.

DESERT FLIER

A man was flying his glider through the Arizona desert one day, when the wind suddenly dropped and he was forced to make a crash-landing. The man crashed into a huge saguaro cactus, but fortunately survived the landing. The pilot got out of the cockpit and began dancing wildly in the sand, overjoyed to still be alive. Unfortunately, the crash had dislodged the cactus which consequently toppled over and squashed the man.

A CLOSE CALL

During a flight from London to New York, the captain told his co-pilot that he had to go to the toilet but would be right back. The co-pilot suddenly had a warning of turbulence ahead and, not feeling confident to fly the plane through turbulence alone, he alerted the captain via an intercom. On getting no response, the co-pilot switched on to auto-pilot and went to check on the captain himself. As he closed the cockpit door behind him, the captain emerged from the toilet. With horror, they discovered that neither of them had the key to the cockpit door. In front of horrified passengers, the two pilots smashed through the door with a fire axe and managed to get through just before the turbulence hit.

THE GOLF COURSE POISONER

A man from Tokyo was on the fifth day of a golfing holiday when he suddenly collapsed and had to be taken to hospital for treatment. The examining doctor eventually diagnosed the man as being poisoned and informed the police of the incident. The detective in charge of the case questioned the man, but could think of no reason why anybody would like to poison him. The detective continued to ask the man questions and eventually was able to deduce that the man had unwittingly poisoned himself. The golfer had the habit of holding the tee between his teeth after teeing off on each hole. The golf course had been heavily sprayed with pesticide, so every time the man took the tee in his mouth, he ingested a small amount of toxic pesticide. Eventually, he poisoned himself.

DEAD AGAIN

In Madrid, Spain, a mortuary attendant was sent out in a hearse to pick up the body of an old man who had died the previous night. The attendant drove out and picked up the body, but on the way back, he heard gurgling noises coming from the back of the hearse. He stopped the car and got out. Unzipping the body bag, the attendant was shocked to discover that the old man was actually still alive. The movement of the car had somehow aroused the man from a coma. The attendant immediately phoned a local hospital and was told to drive toward the hospital and an ambulance would meet him on the way. The attendant, a little shaky after the experience, drove erratically and collided with the ambulance coming the other way. In a cruel twist of fate, the old man was killed.

THE WEDDING

A couple was getting married in a church in Edinburgh, Scotland. The groom was waiting at the pulpit and hundreds of guests were anxiously awaiting the bride's arrival. Eventually, the organist began playing "The Wedding March" and all the guests stood up. The first bridesmaid entered the church, but on her second step down the aisle, she got the heel of her shoe stuck in a grate in the floor. The usher next to her, tried to pull out the shoe, only to pick up the entire grate with it, so to save any embarrassment, he took the grate with him. Unfortunately, the bride, resplendent in her gown and veil, had not noticed and as she glided down the aisle, she fell down the hole the grate had uncovered.

THE PROUD TOURIST

In Hollywood, California, a famous actor was in an ice cream parlour, when an English tourist came in to buy an ice cream. The tourist recognised the actor, but resisting the urge to swoon, stayed calm, bought her ice cream and left without saying a word. However, a few steps out of the shop, she realised that while she had taken her change, she was missing her ice cream. Slightly embarrassed, she returned to the ice cream parlour and asked for her ice cream. The actor stepped up to her and, with a wink, said, "Sister, you'll find your ice cream in your purse, where you put it."

THE IDLE THREAT

A mother from Athens, Greece, had been trying to stop her three-year old son from wetting the bed for over a year without success. She had tried offering him sweets and toys and reading bed-time stories, but the boy kept wetting the bed every night. Exasperated, the woman shouted at the boy, "If you wet your bed again, I'll cut it off!" Unfortunately the boy's seven-year-old sister had overheard her mother's idle threat and taken it literally. The next morning, the sister discovered that her brother had again wet the bed. As her parents were still asleep, she got hold of a pair of scissors and carried out the threat. The poor infant bled to death.

HOME ALONE

A young couple from New York had to go away for a friend's funeral in Los Angeles and, not wanting to expose their ten-month-old baby to such a sad experience, they asked the wife's mother to look after him while they were away. When it was time to leave to catch their plane, the grandmother had still not turned up. The wife rang her grandmother, who told them she was running late and to go for their plane. She would grab a taxi over and be there in ten minutes. Convinced, the couple left their baby in his high chair and hurried to the airport. However, the grandmother, in her rush, had a heart attack and died in her apartment. The couple returned from their trip to find that their son had died of starvation.

FATHER CHRISTMAS

A father from Detroit, Michigan, had always disappointed his family at Christmas by not turning up because of a business meeting or being too tired to join in the festivities. So this year, he was determined to give them a big surprise. He told his wife that he wouldn't be able to make it until Boxing Day, but on Christmas Eve, he dressed up as Santa Claus and climbed on to the roof of his house with a sack of presents. Unfortunately, as he was climbing down the chimney, he got stuck in the flue and choked to death on the soot. Later that night, the family lit the fire, as they did every Christmas Eve, and the room filled with smoke and the stench of burnt flesh. The mother called the police who discovered her roasted husband halfway up the chimney.

THE INFLATABLE BRA

A young Canadian woman, who was paranoid about the smallness of her breasts, was delighted when she came across an inflatable bra that she could "blow up to any size desired". The woman bought the bra and, when a friend invited her to a party, she decided to try it out. At the party, the woman spotted a handsome man in the corner and decided that she must get to know him at all costs. However, as she was about to approach him, she noticed that the man was chatting to a rather buxom woman. The young woman retreated to the bathroom and inflated her bra until she was satisfied that her breasts looked bigger than the other woman's. She then approached the man and immediately attracted his attention away from the other woman. The man eventually asked her if she wanted to dance and she readily agreed. However, the music suddenly increased in tempo and as the man took her in his arms, her bra exploded. The woman fled the party in tears.

LEAP OF FAITH

A hard-working Japanese man was in his office when he received a surprise visit from his wife, who told him that she was leaving him for a professional karaoke singer. Overcome by emotion, the man decided to kill himself by throwing himself out of his office window, which was six floors up. It happened that he threw himself out of the window just as his wife was leaving the building and he landed right on top of her, instantly killing her. The husband survived, but was sentenced to life imprisonment for murder.

LIGHT-FINGERED

A Swedish man, who worked in a saw mill, must have had his thoughts on something else one day when he pushed a plank of wood too far and sliced one of his fingers off. When his colleague asked the man what had happened, he simply put another plank of wood on the saw mill and repeated what he had done, lopping off another finger. Luckily, most of the other workers were off that day or the man might have lost all his fingers.

SPEEDING TYRE

A poor Russian farmer's tractor was on its last legs and the threadbare tyres needed patching yet again. The farmer was inside the tractor tyre patching it, when the tyre began rolling down the hill. Before he knew it, the tyre was rolling at a substantial speed and the farmer became dizzy and disorientated, before blacking out completely. He ended up on a major road, rolling against traffic, causing a few cars to swerve out of the way, but luckily avoided crashing into them. Eventually, the tyre rolled into a field of wheat, slowed down and stopped. When the farmer came to, he realised he had a long walk home and that it was all uphill.

THE TIGHT TROUSERS

A boy from Amsterdam had just passed his test to drive a motorbike and his parents had given him a 250cc bike as a reward. The boy had always dreamt of becoming a biker and he used his savings to buy all the gear - boots, helmet, leather jacket, leather trousers and gloves. None of the shops had his size in leather trousers, but, unable to wait, he bought a larger pair with the idea that he could shrink them. When he got home, he ran a bath and got in still wearing the trousers. Unfortunately, he fell asleep - when he woke up, he was in agony. The leather trousers had shrunk so much, that they had restricted the boy's blood circulation. His mother took him to hospital where they cut the leather trousers away and, finding that the prolonged restriction of blood supply had caused permanent damage, they also had to amputate his legs. The boy's dream of being a cool biker was never to be, but he did have fun racing around in his wheelchair.

ONLY IN HOLLYWOOD

A young actor, trying to make it in Hollywood, was broken-hearted when his first love left him for a film producer. Brought up on the sentimental romanticism of the Hollywood love story, the actor planned to kill himself by taking an overdose of sleeping pills. Before doing so, he took all the love letters from his sweetheart and proceeded to burn them. However, the burning pile soon got out of control and, before he knew it, his whole room was aflame. Overcome by smoke, the actor passed out but, fortunately, the fire brigade came and rescued him. Like a good Hollywood ending, the actor fell in love with the fireman that rescued him and they lived happily ever after.

THE ANNIVERSARY PRESENT

A Welsh man decided that the perfect present for his wife on their 25th anniversary would be if he turned up in a package in the morning post. So, the day before their anniversary, with the help of a neighbour, he packed himself in a large crate and his neighbour took him to the post office and posted him. All might have gone well had there not, first of all, been a postal strike the day of their anniversary and, secondly, a computer error which resulted in the crate being shipped off to Alaska. As it turned out, the husband became a wonderfully successful fisherman and the wife eventually moved in with the neighbour so they all lived happily ever after.

THE ROLLER-SKATER

In London, a boy had been learning the art of roller-skating, when he noticed a lace had come undone. He rested the skate on the bumper of a truck to tighten it up, but the truck suddenly started up and, unable to wrench his skate free, the boy was pulled behind. Unfortunately, the truck was bound for Edinburgh and the poor boy was dragged for over 250 miles on the motorway before the driver decided to stop at the motorway services for a cup of tea. The boy finally managed to break free form the truck's bumper, but now found himself without any money to get home. So he did the obvious thing - crossed over the motorway and latched himself on to a truck going back to London. The boy went on to become one of the fastest roller-skaters in the world.

THE MANUSCRIPT

A French writer had been sweating for years over a piece of writing which had taken eight years to research. During that time the writer had neglected his wife and ruined his social life by devoting all his time to the project. In order to safeguard the precious manuscript he gave it to his wife for her to photocopy. Unfortunately his wife, in a bizarre twist of fate, mistook the paper-shredder for the photocopying machine and every page of the manuscript ended up as scraps of paper. There was nothing for it but for the writer to start all over again.

THE LAST CARRIAGE

A couple was on a dream vacation on the Orient Express from London to Moscow. Early one morning, the man was woken up when the train came to a sudden halt. Unable to go to sleep, he went to use the bathroom, but found it was occupied so, feeling desperate, the man went to use the bathroom on the next carriage. After using the bathroom, he went to return to his carriage, but was horrified to discover that the train had left the carriage he was on behind. Unfortunately, the train company had decided to leave the last carriage behind, because there were no longer any passengers in it. The poor man was stranded half-dressed in Leipzig while his wife was on her way to Moscow.

THE LAST CIGARETTE

A young couple was taking the train from Manchester to London. As the girl didn't smoke, the boy had agreed to sit in a non-smoking carriage and go into the corridor for the occasional cigarette. An hour into the journey, the boy felt the need for a nicotine hit and, telling his girlfriend he would be right back, went into the corridor to light up a cigarette. The girl took a magazine out of her bag and started reading it, glancing over from time to time because she could just make out her boyfriend's legs in the corridor. After a while, the boy hadn't returned so the girl went out to see what he was doing. When she saw what hac happened, she let out a blood-curdling scream. Against all good sense, the boy had leant his head right out of the window and a train, passing the other way, had knocked it right off, leaving his body leaning on the inside for his girlfriend to see.

A PARTY TO DIE FOR

A young man was at Manchester University and living in a shared house with some other students. The students were all getting ready to go to the first big party of the year and the young man was rushing around like a maniac. He was refilling his lighter with gas when a freak spark caused it to explode in his face. Although he wasn't harmed, the ball of fire had scorched his fringe and the young man ran to the bathroom to douse his hair. The other students had got impatient waiting for their friend, so they went up to his room to hurry him along. When they entered, all they saw was a cloud of smoke and a tuft of burnt hair on the floor. They all jumped to the conclusion that their friend had spontaneously combusted. Meanwhile, the young man had washed his hair and when he didn't see his housemates waiting downstairs, decided that they had left without him and ran out the door after them. His housemates stayed in to mourn their friend's mysterious combustion. The young man returned later that night, very much alive and drunkenly merry. Needless to say, when he said, "Wow, what a great party. What happened to you guys?", they lynched him.

HOT LENSES

A man from Huddersfield, Yorkshire, had worked as a welder for most of his life, but had been recently been experiencing headaches and blurred vision. On his wife's advice, he went to the opticians for an eye test and was told he was short-sighted. He told the optician he didn't want to wear glasses, so the optician prescribed him some contact lenses. Wearing his contact lenses, the man was delighted to find he could see things in detail and experienced a new lease of life. However, one day he was doing a particularly tricky piece of welding and removed his goggles so he could see better. Unfortunately, the welding generated so much heat, it caused his contact lenses to fuse to his cornea.

THE PAINTED TOILET

In Dublin, Ireland, the father of a family had just installed a new toilet seat and intended to paint it the colours of the Irish flag - green, white and orange. He painted it green and orange, but ran out of white paint, so he told his wife he was just popping out to the shops. On his way back, however, he decided to stop for a quick pint of Guinness in his local pub. In the meantime, the priest had made an unexpected visit and the mother of the family was entertaining him with tea and biscuits. At one point, the priest asked if he could use the bathroom and the mother directed him upstairs. When the priest hadn't returned after 30 minutes, the mother went to see what had happened to him. The poor priest was stuck fast to the toilet and had been too embarrassed to shout for help. The mother averted her eyes as she helped the priest off the toilet and vowed never to say a word about it, although she did stifle a giggle when she saw the priest's green and orange backside.

A HARD DAY'S NIGHT

A Lithuanian man got drunk at a nightclub after a hard week at the office. Just before the nightclub was due to close, the man went to the toilet to throw up and in the process lost his wedding ring down the toilet. His attempts to retrieve it ended in disaster, when his arm got stuck in the U-bend. His cries for help went unheard as the staff had assumed the man had left and closed up the nightclub. The man had to spend the whole night with his arm stuck down the toilet with his own vomit until cleaners found him the next day. They helped him get his wedding ring back and he went home. The man's wife was so disgusted at the sight and smell of him, she threw her wedding ring at him and demanded a divorce.

BLOW OUT

Some people really should have paid more attention in chemistry class. One such man, a carpenter from Birmingham, was severely injured after he made the most basic of errors. Having spent the day painting and decorating his house, he washed off all the dirt he had accumulated during the course of his day and set to work to remove the paint that had splattered all over his hair and skin. Ignoring the fact that he was burning incense in several different containers placed about the bathroom, he opened a can of petrol that he had siphoned from his car and set about scrubbing away at the paint…for a second or two. Before he knew what had happened, the petrol fumes were ignited by the candle flames in the incense burners. The DIY expert was then blasted out into the street and two of the non-supporting walls in his bathroom were later found to be propping up the bedroom. There was minimal fire damage.

SORRY DARLING

One of the unspoken fears felt by everyone who works in the emergency services is the thought that one day they will arrive at an incident to discover that a loved one is the victim. It is very rarely the case, however, that the emergency services are responsible for the accident in the first place. One such incident occurred when the fire brigade was called out to a fire at a large shop. A large crowd gathered to watch the fire crew extinguish the flames, and even took the trouble to applaud their fine efforts. Having packed away their hoses, the crew jumped back into the fire engine and reversed out on to the street, running over the driver's wife as they did so. The poor woman had been watching her husband at work but had not wanted to put him off by making her presence known. As she stood gripped with awe and wonder at her husband's brave efforts he ran her over.

BAD VIBES

A woman, who had been driving alone through the countryside, was involved in an accident. When it came time to fill in the insurance forms, it emerged that she had been alone at the time and that no other cars were involved. She stated on her accident claim form that she had been driving within the speed limit. Police reports confirmed that driving conditions were almost perfect on the day of the accident. What then could have been the cause of the accident? The insurance company decided to investigate further, but found the woman to be very vague on many of the points put to her. Eventually they contacted the ambulance service and discovered why the woman had been reluctant to answer some of their questions. Apparently, she had crashed the car because she had been using a vibrator at the time of the accident.

ALL SHOT UP

A family in Kentucky was obviously determined to prove Darwin's theory of evolution wrong. However, despite a number of very determined attempts to remove themselves from the gene pool, the family continues to thrive. It all began when father and son went out to hunt squirrels. Armed to the teeth, they went in search of bushy-tailed varmints and were soon rewarded when the son spotted one on a low branch. "There's one," he shouted and both father and son fired at once. Unfortunately, they succeeded only in shooting each other. Meanwhile, back at the ranch, the daughter of the family, who had been watching far too much television, decided that she was going to learn how to twirl a pistol around her finger the way she had seen the gunfighters do it. Clearly not one to do things by half, she used a loaded pistol with the safety catch off and managed to shoot herself in the foot on the first twirl. The second twirl sent a bullet flying through the kitchen window, narrowly missing her mother's arm and hitting her in the chest instead.

FRISBEE FOOL

A man who decided to relive his glory days returned to his old high school – where he had recently been overseeing some building work – with a view to crashing the prom party. Stopping off at a bar on the way to the school, he got well and truly drunk before continuing on his way and arriving just as the party was coming to an end. As is the way with alcohol, he found several like-minded fellows among the students, young men who were in the mood to party. Finding that everyone else was of a mind to go home, the man used his pass key to take his new friends into the brand new, almost finished gym. One of the guys picked up a Frisbee and, without looking where he was going, Mr Glory Days ran towards the other end of the gym shouting "Throw it to me". Before he had the chance to catch the Frisbee, however, he fell down a hole in the flooring that he had failed to cover over in the course of his building work and ended up spending the next six months in a wheel chair.

A ROLLING STONE

An electrician who had been hired by his local council to maintain and repair the borough's street lights ended up in hospital after a well-intentioned passer-by attempted to save him from what appeared to be certain death. While the electrician was high up a ladder trying to rewire one of the street lights, he became bothered by a stone in his shoe. Rather than take the shoe off, he attempted to move the stone by shaking his leg vigorously. A pensioner who was out walking his dog at the time happened to be looking up at the electrician when he did this. Imagining that the poor man's shaking leg was the result of a convulsion brought on by a huge shock of electricity from the street lamp, he did what any sensible person would do and attempted to free the victim from the source of the shock. Unfortunately, this involved kicking the ladder out from under the electrician, an action which resulted in two broken legs and several months off work.

LOOSE MOOSE

Police investigating a hit-and-run accident arrived at the scene of the crime to find a 13-year-old boy and a middle-aged man. Both seemed in a state of distress. When questioned as to what had happened, both witnesses provided statements that the officers found hard to believe. Apparently, the boy had been riding the moped (illegally) when a moose ran out in front of him. The frightened creature leapt into the air and came back down with a crash on the back seat of the moped, knocking the boy off it at the same time. The moped, now being "driven" by the moose, carried on a little way down the road before crashing out of control into an oncoming car. The moose chose this moment to make its getaway. The driver of the car, who ended up with a damaged pelvis, was able to confirm the boy's story (at least the bit about the moose riding the moped). The police officers had little choice but to file a report detailing a hit-and-run accident involving a moped being driven in a dangerous fashion by a moose.

ANIMALS

A characteristic of all decent people is that they can be relied upon to cheer for the underdog. This same trait comes to the fore when we settle down to enjoy a good animal story. Animals, on the whole, are not best equipped to take on humans in a battle of wits – unless we are talking tigers in a jungle, in which case the odds are more favourably stacked. The family pet is always going to be at a disadvantage. So it is all the funnier when they triumph in a comic situation.

We want animals to be funny. It is what makes them seem more human, and by making them more human we allow ourselves to become closer to them. Pets tend to give their owners the kind of unconditional love that is so hard to find in real life. Although this kind of love can be gained from a pet, it becomes all the more valuable if we can give the animal human characteristics, such as fallibility. After all is it not written that to err is human but to forgive is canine?

HAMPERED HAMPSTER

In Glasgow, Scotland, a carpet-layer was just finishing off putting a new carpet in an old woman's lounge, when he noticed a curious lump in the middle. Reluctant to start all over again and remove all the nails, the carpet-layer took his hammer and attempted to flatten the lump. After a few good hits with the hammer and a few stomps with his boot, the carpet looked as good as ever and the carpet-layer packed up his tools. As he was about to leave, the old woman emerged from the kitchen and asked the man, "Before you go, young man, you couldn't help me find my pet hamster, could you?" The carpet-layer mumbled an excuse about being late for another appointment and rushed out the door.

QUIET CAT

In Nashville, Tennessee, a missionary paid a visit on an old woman who was a regular at his church. The old woman told him to sit down in the lounge and then brought him tea and biscuits. The missionary told the woman about his recent work, but he was getting increasingly annoyed with the woman's cat, which kept pulling and chewing on his robe cords. At one point when the woman had gone to make some more tea, the man kicked the cat away. However, he hadn't realised how old the cat was and the kick killed it. Hearing the woman coming back in, the missionary panicked and picked up the cat and put it on his lap and began stroking it. The old woman didn't seem to notice and they continued their conversation. The missionary finished his cup of tea and wished the old lady good health and left. A few days later, the old lady turned up at the church and took the missionary aside. With a tear in her eye, she said, "I hate to tell you this, because you seemed to be getting on so well, but my cat passed away soon after you left."

A DOG'S LIFE

A man from Connecticut had to relocate to New York City because of his job. Although he could only find an apartment in a high rise in Upper Manhattan, he was loath to leave his faithful dog behind and so he took her with him, vowing to take her for long walks through the park at least twice a day. The man moved in with his dog and everything seemed to work for a few weeks. So much so, in fact, that the man invited his brother's family for a weekend visit. The brother brought his wife and their seven-year-old son, who was particularly overjoyed to see the dog. The boy played with the dog in the apartment, but he got a little over-enthusiastic while throwing a tennis ball. The boy threw the ball which ricocheted off the wall and straight out the window. The dog, probably not used to its new city life, trotted eagerly after the ball, following it out the window and down something in the region of 23 floors.

REINCARNATED RABBIT

A man living in the suburban outskirts of London was used to his dog digging up old bones and objects and bringing them into the house, but he was most upset when his dog brought in the neighbour's pet rabbit looking very limp and, as it turns out, very dead. His neighbours had gone on holiday for a week and, not feeling able to face the prospect of confessing his dog's misdemeanor, he sneaked into their back garden and replaced the lifeless rabbit in its hutch. A few days after the neighbours returned, he bumped into the husband and after several pleasantries, he discreetly asked after the rabbit. "Funny thing that," said his neighbour, "our rabbit died just before we went away and we buried it in the garden, but when we got back some sick joker had dug it up and put it back in its hutch!"

ARACHNOPHOBIA

A Californian woman returned from shopping one day and was unpacking her groceries when she saw, among a bunch of bananas, what looked like a spider. Only that morning, the woman had heard on the radio about the risks of bringing in poisonous spiders in shipments of fruit from South America. The size of the thing convinced the woman it was a bird-eating spider and she slowly backed away towards the back door. Shutting it behind her, she ran to her next-door neighbour, told her what had happened and her neighbour phoned the police. Not long after, the police evacuated the whole area, firemen pumped toxic gases into the woman's house and experts from the local zoo began a thorough search of the premises. Five minutes after the team had entered the house, they emerged, angry looks on their faces – the dangerous spider had turned out to be a harmless black wig that had somehow fallen into the old woman's groceries.

DINNER TIME

One summer, a science student at a London University woke up every day at dawn and went to the Arsenal football ground when noone was around. He always wore a black top and black shorts and he would scatter birdseed while walking up and down the pitch for about 20 minutes, finishing his visit with a sharp blast from a football whistle. In August, it was time for the first football game of the season and Arsenal were playing Chelsea. The referee tossed a coin and Arsenal decided to kick off. When the referee blew his whistle, however, thousands of birds suddenly descended on to the pitch like a scene out of Alfred Hitchcock's The Birds. The game was postponed for an hour as stewards ran around trying to clear the field of the birds. The science student graduated on the basis of his study on the feeding patterns of the common sparrow.

HARD CHICKENS

The British Aviation Authority used to test the strength of windshields on planes using a device that could fire out dead chickens at extremely high speed. The device was pointed at the aircraft's windshield and if the chicken didn't break it, it was assumed that the windshield would survive the impacts of actual collisions with birds when in flight. British Rail had recently designed a new locomotive and was testing various designs of windshields, so they borrowed the device from the BAA. Adjusting it to approximate the maximum speed of the train, they loaded a dead chicken and fired it at the first windshield design. The chicken went straight through the windshield, broke several components and left a huge dent in the compartment door. Surprised by the result, they asked a BAA official if they had done the test correctly. An engineer checked everything and suggested that for their next test they defrost the chicken.

HUMAN ZOO

A mother took her 14-year-old son to the doctor after he complained of stomach cramps. Examining the boy, the doctor realized it was serious and immediately sent him to hospital to have his stomach pumped out. At the hospital, the mother waited anxiously, cringing every time she heard her son gag in the room next door. After 15 minutes of this, a nurse came out and told the mother she could go in to her son. She took the boy in her arms as soon as she saw he was basically okay, although a bit traumatized. The doctor took the mother aside and showed her what had been causing the stomach cramps. She nearly fainted when she saw a container full of tiny crabs scurrying around. The only explanation she could come up with was that they had gone to the beach a few days before and her son must have swallowed some water whilst swimming. Crab eggs in the water then incubated and hatched in the poor boy's stomach.

DOG AND PHONE

A man from Manchester, England became frantic when he couldn't find his mobile phone anywhere in his house. He had looked everywhere and even phoned the number from his house phone in the hope of hearing the mobile ringing somewhere. Soon after he'd tried phoning the mobile, his wife returned home from walking the dog. She looked very concerned. She'd been playing fetch with Jessie, a 30kg St Bernard, when she heard a strange, muffled ringing sound coming from somewhere nearby. After realizing that the ringing became louder when Jessie approached her, she'd put her head to the dog's stomach and discovered the ringing was coming from Jessie. Worried, she returned straight home. The man was delighted that the phone had been found, but a little bemused as to how to retrieve it and, like his wife, was concerned for Jessie's health and well-being. He called the veterinary surgeon who told him the best thing to do was to wait for time – and the phone – to pass. They took the dog for another walk and sure enough, half an hour later, the phone popped out.

RAINING WHALEMEAT

An eight ton, 45-foot sperm whale, dead for some time, washed up on the Pacific Ocean beach in Oregon. Initially, it was a curiosity for local residents and visitors, but soon the foul smell of rotting whale pervaded the area and became unbearable. The authorities thought that if they buried the carcass, it would probably just get uncovered by the tide – so after much discussion it was decided to blast the blubber to bits using dynamite. Unfortunately, the explosives experts miscalculated the amount of dynamite needed and the resulting explosion sent pieces of blubber raining down over a stunned crowd of curious spectators that had gathered. The authorities were forced to organize a task force to comb the area, collect all the pieces of blubber and burn the lot. It took six days to complete the job.

TRUNK CALLS

The people living in a small village on the edge of the jungle of southern India domesticated a female elephant to help with their logging activities. The elephant was named Madhu and when not working, was chained to a tree. Although it's unusual for wild elephants to be attracted to domesticated elephants, for one three-ton bull elephant it was love at first sight and he wouldn't leave Madhu's side. At first, the villagers tried to lure the huge beast away with bananas, but when that failed, they tried intimidating it by shouting and throwing firecrackers. This worked, in that it drove the animal back into the jungle, but not before it left a trail of demolished huts in its wake. Still consumed with love, the bull elephant sneaked back into the village that night and freed Madhu by breaking her chains, and the two lovers eloped back into the jungle.

SEX TOY

One winter, a wooden deer, used for target practice near an Alaskan village attracted the attention of a wild bull moose. Undeterred by the pockmarks in the life-sized model, the bull made several passionate passes as amused hunters watched from a safe distance. The brief affair ended when the bull's advances became increasingly physical. The bull didn't seem to notice when the deer's antlers broke off, but when its head fell off, he stopped abruptly and dismounted the decapitated deer. The frustrated bull moose looked down at the broken head, snorted and trotted off back to the woods.

POODLE SOUP

A wealthy old woman was taking her poodle for a walk in the park, but she and her dog got soaked in a sudden downpour. On returning home, the eccentric old woman, feeling sorry for her poor cherub, had a wonderful idea of how to dry him. She went straight into the kitchen and popped her unsuspecting dog in the microwave oven. After trying to comfort the poor, whimpering creature, the woman closed the door, set it for three minutes and turned it on. She had just put on the kettle on for a cup of tea when the poodle exploded. She no doubt needed the cup of tea, or maybe something a little stronger...

DIVING DOGGIE

Two boys were walking in the woods when they came across a cottage in a clearing. Seeing that it was deserted, they went to investigate and discovered an old, overgrown well. Being at that curious age, they decided to find out how deep it was, so one boy picked up a stone and dropped it down the well. After what seemed like forever, there was a quiet splash as the stone hit the bottom. The other boy then found a bigger stone and dropped it down the well – the splash was a little louder this time. The boys began looking for bigger and bigger rocks to make louder and louder splashes. Eventually, one boy found a large metal spike in the ground and pulled it out and, with a big grin, he threw it down the well. They then noticed that the spike was attached to a long chain that was now rattling through the long grass and into the well. The chain gathered momentum until suddenly, a tethered dog, scared out of its wits, burst through the bushes, whizzed past them and went hurtling down the well.

PECKER PECKS PECKER...

A man who was fond of birds of prey developed a ritual: every time he left his local bar in the evening he would take a small sausage out of his pocket and hold it up in the air. Before too long, an owl would swoop down from the trees and grab the sausage out of his hand. One night, after one too many beers, the man staggered out of the pub, and was so drunk that he forgot to take the sausage out of his pocket. Feeling a sudden need to take a leak, he went behind a tree and took his pecker out. The confused owl swooped down and grabbed the poor man's member in its talons. The man swore he'd never drink again.

CANINE SURPRISE

A man who was particularly fond of steak pies couldn't resist an offer on The Ultimate Prime Steak Pie at a marked-down price in his local supermarket. That evening, excited about digging into the huge pie, he warmed it up, cooked some vegetables and got out a few beers. Sitting down to eat, he licked his lips, took his time and savoured every mouthful, only pausing now and then to take a swig of beer. He had nearly eaten most of the pie, when his fork hit something metallic. He choked on his beer when he pulled out a dog tag with the inscription: "If you find our darling Princess, please call this number". After that night, the man gave up eating meat and became a staunch vegetarian.

NOT GUILTY

Two men were driving up to a lodge in the mountains for a weekend of deer hunting, when they realized they were lost. Spotting a farm up ahead, the driver stopped the car, telling his friend to wait while he asked for directions. At the farmhouse, he came across a distressed farmer who told the hunter that his horse was ill and needed to be put down. The farmer explained that he had become too fond of the horse to kill it himself, and on learning that the man was a hunter asked him to shoot the horse. At first, the man refused, but the farmer continued to plead with him and he eventually relented. The farmer showed the man the horse and gave him a rifle. The man shot the horse, the farmer thanked him and told him the way to the lodge. As he returned to the car, the man decided to play a joke on his companion. He explained that the farmer was so rude, that he shot his horse. Instantly, his friend grabbed a rifle from the back of the car and disappeared. Soon after there were two gunshots and then the friend ran back, jumped in the car and said: "That'll teach him. I shot two of his cows."

CAT RETIREMENT

A wealthy woman, living in the heart of Paris, had a cat that was very precious to her. The cat was getting old and the woman decided that the least she could do was move out to the country for the final years of the cat's life, so the he could enjoy the space and tranquillity away from the noise and smog of the city. Eventually, the woman moved into a small farmhouse in a village just outside Paris. After unpacking, the woman put the cat on the grass to soak up the sun and, while she talked to him, she prepared his dinner in the kitchen. Suddenly she was alarmed to hear the cat squeal in pain and ran outside, just in time to see a falcon flying off with her beloved cat in its claws.

THE PAINTED DOG

In Zurich, Switzerland, a teenage boy took his father's car without permission and crashed it. For some months the father's mother had been asking her grandson if he could paint her lounge and the father saw this as an appropriate punishment for his son. Consequently, the following weekend the father left his son at his mother's house with a can of yellow paint and a paintbrush. The son went about the task with an enthusiastic relish and finished quite quickly. He stepped back to admire the work, but kicked the can of paint all over a priceless Persian rug. The boy knew he would be in an enormous amount of trouble, but just then he heard the yapping of his grandmother's Chihuahua. He grabbed the dog and dropped her in the middle of the spilt paint while shouting loudly, "Oh, no! You bad, bad dog!" The boy got away with the deed, but the grandmother punished her dog by not feeding it for three days.

SIT!

In Florence, Italy, a young man thought he had struck gold when a girl from a rich family invited him round to meet her parents. The boy dressed up in his best suit and arrived early to make a good impression. The young man could hardly contain his excitement when he saw the family's huge mansion. The door was answered by a butler, who showed him into a room and told him to make himself comfortable. Spotting a sumptuous leather armchair, the boy leaped into it, only to hear a loud series of cracks. The young man quickly got up to see what had made the sound. His worse fears were substantiated when he discovered he had sat on the family Pekinese dog and broken its neck. Not knowing what else to do, the young man hid the dead dog under the leaves of a large pot plant and ran off.

CITY SLICKER

A city man from Wellington decided to take a weekend break in the country hunting deer. He drove out until he came across a farm and asked the farmer if he could hunt on his land. The farmer told the man he could hunt as long as steered clear of his prize bull which was worth $3,000. A few hours later, the city man returned to the farmer and, shaking his head, nervously told him that he had shot his bull by mistake. Without another word, the man wrote out a cheque for $3,500, gave it to the farmer and left. The farmer went to look at his prize bull and was more than delighted when he found it completely undisturbed, grazing in its pasture. Searching the rest of his farm, he discovered the body of a buck. The city man had been too thick to know the difference between a bull and a deer. The farmer couldn't believe his luck - $3,500 the richer and three weeks worth of venison.

THE VISIT

In Waterford, Ireland, a local priest was making the usual rounds of his parish. A family had just moved into the area and the priest was eager to make a good first impression to welcome them. As the priest approached the family's house, he noticed a large, playful dog in the front garden and gave it a friendly pat. When the woman of the house invited the priest inside, the dog followed him in. The priest was shown into the lounge where the father and their three children were sitting. The priest attempted to make polite conversation, but was thwarted by the dog's antics. The dog smelled like it hadn't been washed in months, tracked mud all over the carpet and furniture and gobbled up some biscuits that the mother had thoughtfully provided. The priest decided it might be best to leave before the dog becomes even more embarrassing. As he headed towards the door, the mother remarked coldly, "Don't forget your dog, Father." "My dog?" the priest exclaimed, "Isn't he yours?!"

THE PUPPY

In Chester, England, a young girl was thrilled to get a puppy for her birthday. She played with it for hours and then decided to take him for a walk. Before leaving the house, her mother told her to keep an eye on her pet and not to let him go because he was not familiar enough with the area. The girl took her puppy for a walk around the house, and then remembered that she had a tennis ball inside for him to play with. The girl tied the puppy to the handle of the garage door and ran in to get the ball. Just then, the girl's father arrived home and, as he turned the car into the driveway, he hit the remote control to open the garage door. As the door opened, it pulled the tied puppy into the air, choking it. Fortunately, the father heard the puppy's squeals and untied him just in time.

THE DEAD POODLE

A baggage handler at Charles de Gaulle Airport in Paris, was horrified to discover a dead poodle in a crate bound for Berlin. Worried that he would be blamed for neglecting the animal, the baggage handler frantically rushed around the city hunting through the pet shops. Finally he found, and bought, an identical poodle. The relieved baggage handler put the poodle in a crate on the next flight to Berlin. The poodle's owner was an old German lady, who was very annoyed when she was informed that her poodle had been put on the next flight by mistake. However, when the crate finally arrived a few hours later, the old lady fainted as the lively poodle yapped at her. It seems that her own poodle had died while on holiday in Paris and she was shipping it back to Berlin for burial.

THE KITTEN THAT FELL OUT OF THE SKY

In Berkeley, California, a woman decided to take a kitten as a pet. Some weeks later, the woman was doing some gardening, when she heard the kitten miaowing. She saw that it had climbed to the highest branch of a tree and no manner of coaxing could persuade it to climb down. The woman tried looping a rope around the end of the branch, hoping to pull it down so that she could reach the kitten. Unfortunately, as she pulled on the rope, it snapped, and the branch sprang back, launching the miaowing kitten into the air. The woman searched all over the place but couldn't find it. The distraught woman spent days knocking on peoples' doors in the area until one morning, an old man answered her knock. The woman explained what had happened to her kitten and asked if the man had seen it. The man smiled and said, "So that's where the little bugger came from. I was minding my own business, sitting in the back garden, when this kitten drops out of the sky and into my lap! Gave me the fright of my life!" The man went back into his house and returned with the miaowing kitten.

BLUEBERRY CAT

A woman from Richmond, Virginia, had just baked a blueberry pie and set it on the table to cool, when her two sons came home from school. The mother told them she was just going to visit the woman next door and they were not to touch the pie as it was for dessert later. The boys helped themselves to a cold drink and were about to go outside and play, when the lure of the freshly-baked blueberry pie pulled them back and they decided to risk a small bite. However, one small bite led to several and soon they had consumed a whole quarter of the pie. When they heard their mother returning, they had to think quickly and, spotting the cat drinking its milk in the corner, they grabbed it, plonked its face into the middle of the pie and ran out of the kitchen. The mother entered the kitchen, saw the cat on the table with its whiskered covered in crumbs and blueberries and, in an outburst of anger, picked the cat up and threw it out of the window. The unfortunate cat landed in the road, right in front of a passing school bus.

THE HUNTER

A man from Quebec, Canada, went on a hunting trip in the country. The day went badly. He spotted a few deer, but missed each one. When it started to get dark, the man decided to call it a day and drove home. On the way home, the man was delighted when a deer ran into the road in front of him and he ran into it. Although illegal, the man put the deer over his bonnet and continued to drive home. A few miles down the road, however, the deer recovered and began thrashing around. The man grabbed a metal rod from under his seat and swung at the deer, still steering his car. Unfortunately, he caught his faithful hunting dog in mid-swing and the dog bit him. The man brought the car to a halt, leapt out and ran down the road, his angry dog chasing him. The man came across a telephone box and shutting himself inside, he dialled the emergency services. He explained to the operator that he was trapped inside the telephone box by a ferocious dog while a deer was smashing his car. He begged the operator to send a policeman to shoot the animals and save him. The police rescued the man without having to resort to killing the animals, but the man never went hunting again.

THE LIZARD

A little girl came across what she took to be a small lizard in Regent's Park, London, and took it home with her. She put it in a tank where she kept terrapins only to discover an hour later that the "lizard" had eaten them. When the upset girl told her mother, she immediately took the creature to London Zoo for examination. The creature turned out to be a baby Caiman crocodile which could grow up to 8-foot-long in its wild habitat.

DAMP SQUID

The New Zealand coast guard reported sightings of a rare giant squid off the coast of Kaikoura on the South Island. Hundreds of fishermen and scientists went out to either catch or take photographs of the elusive creature. One fisherman eventually spotted the squid and chased it for miles before finally netting it. The proud fisherman was looking forward to a life of fame and fortune, when he was shocked to hear the giant squid say, "Hey, you stupid sod, get me out of this bloody net!" The "squid" was, in fact, an amateur photographer had made and put on a giant squid suit in a bid to attract the attentions of the real creature which he was convinced lived in the area.

THE BANANA BUNCH

In Southampton, England, a woman was doing her weekly grocery shopping when she spotted some imported Guatemalan bananas. A big fan of Central American bananas, the woman picked out several bunches. As she picked up one bunch, she felt a tingling sensation in her hand, but thought nothing of it and paid for the bananas. As the woman was loading the groceries into her car, she suddenly felt dizzy and collapsed. The poor woman died before she reached the hospital. The coroner was intrigued to discover that the woman had been the victim of a poisonous snake bite and, when the police found out that she had just purchased some Guatamalan bananas, they concluded that the snake must've been hidden among the fruits. The snake was never found and, to this day, people believe there are poisonous snakes in Southampton.

BETSY THE ELEPHANT

In Budapest, Hungary, a travelling circus had set up in a large park in the old part of the city. To encourage people to come and see the circus, the owners decided to lead a procession through the streets. It was a huge one, with jugglers, clowns, acrobats, seals on floats, lions in cages and the star attraction, Betsy the elephant. The residents were cheering and applauding until suddenly, Betsy broke free of her chains and stormed into the crowd. Apparently, she had mistaken a small red car parked by the side of the street for a stool used in the circus act, and had run over to balance on it.

THE DODGY CURRY

A woman from London invited some friends around for dinner one night. She had intended to cook a chicken curry, but she was worried that the chicken breast might be off. As a test, she gave a little piece to her cat to see if he would touch it. She was relieved to see him gobble it down without hesitation and went on to make the curry. Later on, her friends were complimenting her on how good her chicken curry was. Pleased, the woman went into the kitchen to prepare the dessert, only to see her cat choking in the corner. The woman hurried back to tell her friends what happened and advised them to go to the hospital to have their stomachs pumped, which they did. She took her cat to the vet for emergency treatment. On examining the cat, the vet said, "My dear lady, this cat is perfectly fine. He just had a hairball in his throat."

THE CAT UP THE TREE

In Chichester, England, an old lady called the fire brigade when her cat got stuck up a tall tree and wouldn't come down. As there was a strike on at the time, a group of volunteers turned up in the fire engine. Although this was the first cat they had had to rescue, they managed it without mishap and the old lady made them all a cup of tea as a way of thanks. When the volunteers went to drive off, however, they didn't see the cat under the wheels of the fire engine and they ran over the poor moggy.

THE HOMESICK CAT

An old man from Hanover, Germany, had put up with his temperamental cat for long enough. He was fed up with her scratching all the furniture and peeing all over the place, so he gave her to a friend, who lived on the other side of town, with the excuse that he was getting too old to look after her. A week later, on a particularly harsh winter's day, the old man returned home from shopping and was surprised to see the cat shivering on his doorstep. Moved by the fact the cat had found her way back from the other side of town in such cold weather, the man took the cat inside and gave her plenty of loving attention. The next day, however, he ran into another friend, who asked him if he had found his cat. The old man said he had and asked what the other man knew about it. The friend replied, "Oh, well, I was on the other side of town, when I recognised your cat in the road, so although she was hissing and struggling all the way, I drove her home and left her on your doorstep."

THE GIANT CLAM

A man went on a diving holiday to Thailand and was having a wonderful time exploring the beautiful underwater scenery of the sea. On one dive, he came across a cave and, on further investigation, spotted a giant clam inside. Realising that the clam could be worth a lot of money, the man approached it, knife in hand, but as he went to prise the clam off the rock, it slammed shut on his other hand. He tried prising the clam open with his knife, but without success. Realising that if he didn't free himself soon, he would run out of air and drown, the man took the only option he had left. He cut his hand off with his knife and just managed to swim to the surface before his air ran out.

ONE FOR THE ROAD

A herd of cows created havoc in a small town in the American Mid-West when they broke out of their paddock. The townspeople were stunned to see the cows staggering down the road, mooing loudly, urinating against walls and flirting with local bulls. After the cows were eventually rounded up, it came to light that the cows were actually quite drunk. It seems the cows had been fed on waste beer from a local brewery. The farmer explained that beer contains vital nutrients and is an excellent supplement to their diet. However, the farmer had not anticipated the effect of alcohol on his herd and he said that he would have to teach them to hold their drink better.

MISTAKEN IDENTITY

This is a case of bureaucracy gone mad. A man, who lived by a small river in Wyoming, informed his local authority that a dam built by beavers had been causing flooding on his land. In due course, the man received a letter telling him that the local authority was prosecuting him for unauthorised construction on the river. The baffled man wrote back, saying that it was actually beavers that had built a dam and that was what he was complaining about. The man didn't hear anything for a month until one morning, two bailiffs knocked on his door and asked him if he knew where a Mr Beaver lived. Apparently, the local authority had fined the beavers $10,000 for the unauthorised construction and another $1,000 for not showing up in court.

THE GREAT ESCAPE

Two pigs, about to be slaughtered, escaped from an abattoir recently. The pigs, thought to be in love, dug a hole under a fence, crept through and swam across the River Avon, to escape certain death at the hands of merciless farmers. Following a nationwide hunt, widely reported in the media, an anonymous animal lover offered to buy the pigs for thousands of pounds to save their bacon. The pigs were eventually discovered hiding out in an abandoned church in deepest, darkest Somerset. The pig farmer, surprised at the turn of events and happy to make such a huge profit, passed the pigs on to their new benefactor.

THE DREADED NEST

With dreadlocks all the rage at the moment, this experience would convince anyone to shave all their hair off. A Californian surfer dude, with a lovely set of dreadlocks, decided that they needed tightening up and paid a visit to the hairdressers. Taking his seat, the dude started talking about a party he was looking forward to that night, but the hairdresser just complimented him on his excellent set of dreads and began to trim them. When the unlucky hairdresser cut into one particularly lumpy dread, hundreds of tiny black widows came scampering out. It took a lot of deduction for the detectives to solve the double murder mystery of the dead surfer and the hairdresser.

MAN'S BEST FRIEND

A farmer in the Australian outback realised that his 12-year-old dog, who was painfully sick, would have to be put down. Unable to bring himself to shoot the poor animal, he came up with an idea. He tied the dog up to a small tree and put a lit stick of dynamite in its mouth. Tears welled up in his eyes as he backed away from the dog and, unable to watch any more, he retreated into the farmhouse. Thirty seconds later, the man had just helped himself to a beer, when he heard the all-too familiar whining at the front door.

HOLIDAY SOUVENIR

This is a classic but it seems to be a common occurrence. A family from Auckland, New Zealand, was on holiday in Thailand. During their stay, they came across a small dog and, when the children fell in love with it, the parents decided to sneak it back home. Having successfully smuggled the puppy through New Zealand customs in the wife's handbag, the family set up a home for the puppy. They gave it a bed and bought it it's very own food and water bowls. A few days later, however, they were horrified to discover their next-door-neighbour's cat had captured and killed their little darling. The family were even more horrified when the vet told them that their darling puppy was in fact a giant Thai rat.

A PLEASANT SURPRISE

An intrepid hunter from Derbyshire was particularly pleased with his catch one weekend. He had bagged an enormous pheasant and so he went down to his local pub to celebrate and show off his prize. After a few pints, the proud hunter took his mates out to his truck and showed them his catch. However, the man, a bit worse for wear from alcohol, stumbled and lost his grip on the dead pheasant. The pheasant knocked the man's gun resting on the side of the truck, causing it to shoot the man in the foot. Forced to report the incident, the man not only lost his regular job because of his incapacitated foot, but he was also fined for shooting pheasant out of season. The pheasants had the last laugh that weekend.

HORSE MEAT

A Spanish farmer had hit hard times. To keep things going, he decided to sell his prize stallion. The farmer was so poor even getting to the market place would be a problem. He had to borrow a car from a neighbour and use a trailer that had been rotting in the corner of the stable for years. Nevertheless, he made the trailer as sturdy as he could, secured his horse inside and started off. Unfortunately for the horse, the farmer's carpentry skills were not so hot. When the trailer went over a bump, the poor horse plunged through the rotten floorboards and was forced to gallop all the way to the market place. When the farmer opened the trailer, he was devastated to see his prize stallion collapsed in a heap. Not surprisingly, the farmer was unable to sell his steed, although he declined an offer from a merciless butcher.

FLAT CAT

A woman was driving home from work late one night, when a cat ran out into the middle of the road. The woman tried to avoid the foolish cat, but when she felt a bump she realised she'd hit it. She got out and found the cat behind her front wheel. Picking it up, she noticed the cat's tag had a phone number on it and decided the least she could do was call the owner. Finding a nearby phone box, the woman called the number and an old lady answered it. The woman told the old lady what had happened. The old lady then asked the woman to describe the cat. "Well," the woman hesitantly replied, "it's mottled brown, rather bloody and flat as a pancake." The old lady said, "Oh, no, you must be mistaken, my dear, my cat doesn't look like that at all," and hung up.

THE MAN-HUNT

An English country squire, frustrated by a recent series of fox hunts and thwarted by hunt saboteurs, decided to do the next hunt without a fox. He engaged a young local man to make a trail of aniseed through the fields and forests. The young man did just that, making an elaborate trail for the fox hounds to follow, and then retired to the local pub to spend the money the squire had given him. A few pints later, the young man was surprised to hear the barking of fox hounds drawing closer, as he had made the aniseed trail lead back to the squire's estate, a few miles away. As he ventured out to investigate, it slowly dawned on him why the fox hounds were coming his way - he stank of aniseed! The man ran for his life, but the hounds soon caught up with him, and subsequently licked him to death. The country squire's weekly sport of man-hunting has since proved extremely popular with fellow red coats.

A FISH OUT OF WATER

A wildlife television crew had been commissioned to document the life of a salmon. The project was to take six months and follow the salmon's progress. They caught a salmon in the sea and without harming it, attached a radio transmitter to it, so they could track it up river where it would lay its eggs. After two months of tracking and filming the salmon's movements, the crew was excited because the fish was about to make its amazing trip upriver. They were startled, however, when the signal suddenly veered away from the river and through a forest. Thinking they had discovered a freak tributary of the river, the crew set about following the signal. After an hour, they stumbled across a campsite and a fire surrounded by a group of boy scouts. On the fire, their precious salmon was being barbecued to perfection.

CREEPY CRAWLY

Although this classic urban myth cannot possibly be true, it has horrified more than enough people. A French woman, who had just returned from a week-long camping trip in the countryside, consulted a doctor about a terrible earache she had. On examining her, the doctor discovered that an earwig had crawled inside the woman's ear. He told her that he couldn't reach the earwig and it would be best to wait for it to come out the other side. A week later, the woman called on the doctor to thank him as the earwig had indeed come out the other ear. To be on the safe side, the doctor re-examined her ears. After the examination, the doctor told the woman, "Unfortunately, the earwig has laid eggs in your head and when they hatch, they'll slowly eat your brain. I'm afraid there's nothing that can be done."

FATAL SHOT

A rugged old man was out hunting in the forests of South Africa when he heard a loud rustling in the trees above. Deciding it must be a large bird, the man lets off a volley of shots into the foliage. As nothing seemed to result from his shooting, the man moved under the tree and when he heard yet more rustling directly overhead, he let off another volley of shots. This time, he was delighted to hear an animal cry out in pain. However, his joy soon turned to despair, when tumbling at speed towards him was a large porcupine. The spiky creature landed right on his face, causing so many lacerations that the man died.

THE CURSE OF THE RATTLESNAKE

A cowboy walking through the Grand Canyon came across a rattlesnake on the path and, after stunning it with his belt, he stomped on its head with his boot. The cowboy returned to his lodge, but within a day, became sick and died. The cowboy's brother inherited his boots, but he also became sick and died. The boots were too small for the other brother, so an uncle took them - when he wore them he became sick and died. The surviving brother, at last making the connection with the boots, examined them and discovered the rattlesnake's fangs embedded in the sole, still with venom on them.

MILKY, MILKY

In a small village in the republic of Azerbaijan, a woman had taken her baby son with her to do some fruit picking. After breast-feeding her baby she left him asleep in his basket and went about filling a bag full of berries. On returning to her baby, the woman was horrified to discover a snake creeping down the infant's throat and choking him. She immediately took the child to a local hospital whereupon they were able to remove the invasive snake. The doctor told the woman that the scent of milk must have lured the snake to her baby.

BUNNY CAT

Anyone who understands the joys of rabbit ownership will know that, despite their incredible cuteness, they are not always the most affectionate or exciting of creatures. Now a company in America is offering to sell a new hybrid animal which, they claim, combines the finest qualities of the rabbit and the cat. Male rabbits are famed for their willingness to attempt sex with any female creature, regardless of species, and by a coincidence rabbits and cats share the same number of chromosomes and a remarkably similar gestation period. Allied to this is the fact that female cats will quite happily raise the young of almost any species as one of their own. All these factors have combined to help animal breeders develop this brand new pet. Called a racat (although some breeders are pushing for the far more attractive name of cabbit) the animal can be ordered from most large pet stores but may take a little while to arrive due to the almost legendarily laid-back nature of both cats and rabbits.

CUPBOARD LOVE

A body of an elderly man was discovered in the Netherlands after it had lain undiscovered for several weeks. When police arrived at the house of the Dutch pensioner to investigate reports of strange smells that had been bothering the neighbours, they discovered 15 apparently healthy and happy cats running about the place, apparently having the time of their lives. The man was not known to be an animal lover and the mystery of why there should be so many cats running around his house was cleared up when officers discovered a broken downstairs window through which the cats had gained access to the man's house. When they went upstairs, however, they discovered why his house had become such a haunt for the felines. He may not have fed any cats while he was alive, but the dead man was now feeding all 15.

BARKING MAD

A couple in Birmingham, England gave the staff of an animal rescue centre in the city great cause for concern when they rang to say that they felt they could no longer look after their 13-year-old family pet, called "Rover". The animal rescuers, who are often called upon to deal with such cases, requested that the couple bring the pet in to the centre, and they would try to find a new home for it. The couple refused, but gave their address and so the rescuers climbed in a van and went over to the couple's house in order to pick up their unwanted pet. Despite frosty looks all round, they were shown in and taken to the room where the pet was being kept, only to discover that "Rover" was in fact a crocodile. The couple appeared to have no idea that the crocodile was dangerous, and even allowed it to sleep in the same room as them.

CRIME

Crime is such a part of our everyday lives that it is inevitable that stories will circulate concerning the near mythical activities of certain criminals. These people, rather than appearing as the lowlifes they actually are, become transformed into heroes. This is because there is a part of all of us that would like to carry out the perfect crime; one with no victims and no consequences. The nearest most of us get to achieving this is to experience the thrill at a distance, when we hear a tale of how someone has pulled off the greatest bank robbery in history, or conned the government out of millions that might otherwise have been spent on pointless projects.

The other major aspect of crime stories is the, often, breathtaking stupidity of those who set out to commit the mythical perfect crime. We cannot help but be entertained by tales of how everything was planned down to the last detail, only for the crime to go horribly wrong after someone did something stupid. Such as forgetting to put fuel in the getaway car, or handing over a demand for lots of money that is written on the back of an envelope addressed to the robber.

What follows are a series of tales of the over ambitious, the seriously stupid or those poor souls who were just plain unlucky. Remember them next time you plan the perfect crime.

A BIT BELOW THE BELT

Police in Lima, Peru, are concerned at a spate of unusual attacks on women in a city car park. Each woman reported that they had left their cars in the car park to go shopping. On their return, as the woman opened her car door, she felt an intense pain across her ankles and on looking down, she saw that a man hiding under the car had slashed her with a knife. The man then emerged from under the car, took all the woman's shopping and drove off in her car. The police have now issued a warning to all women that they should look under their cars before approaching them.

A VERY GOOD YEAR

A man from Swansea, Wales, was shocked to find that his car had been broken into while he popped into the off licence for less than ten minutes. He was slightly amused, however, to find that his car stereo was untouched and the only thing missing was a used wine bottle that contained a urine sample, which he was intending to drop off at his doctor's.

THE THIEVER OF THE BRIDE

In Springfield, Ohio, a wedding reception party was tarnished when it was discovered that someone had been picked the pockets of several guests and stolen their wallets. However, on returning from their honeymoon, the newly-weds invited several people round to watch the wedding video. Halfway through the video, the husband's father jumped up and rewound the tape and played it again. "Aha!" he cried, "There's the thief!" There are on video was the wife's father pinching somebody's wallet. Red-faced, he complained, "How else was I supposed to pay for that damned wedding?"

CHICKEN PICKING

A woman from Helsinki, Finland, was out shopping, but she didn't have enough money for a frozen chicken she needed for a very special dinner that evening. Desperate, the woman hid the frozen chicken under her hat and joined the queue to pay for the vegetables she'd picked up. The queue seemed to take longer than ever and the woman began shiver with cold. As it came to her turn, the woman fainted from the cold and the frozen chicken rolled out from under the hat and came to rest at the store manager's feet.

BABY BALL

In Albuquerque, New Mexico, a woman, who was seven-months pregnant, was shopping for a toy for her two-year-old daughter. She found a doll and paid for it, but as she went to leave, a security guard pulled her aside and asked her to follow him. The security guard took the woman and her daughter to a room in the back. He said, "I believe you have a basketball under your dress." The woman began to protest, but the guard just said, "No, don't give me any of that pregnant stuff, I've heard it all before." The woman had to take her dress off before the security guard was convinced of her pregnancy. She later won a libel suit against the shop for putting her through such an experience.

DIRTY MONEY

In Las Vegas, a blackjack dealer lost his job when he tested positive for cocaine in a random drugs test. The dealer vehemently denied the charge and a industrial tribunal took up his case. After several weeks of investigations and talks, it was soon discovered that most of the dealers in the casino tested positive in the drugs test. It turned out that the dealers weren't using cocaine at all. But customers who abused the substance were using $20 bills to snort the powder and then losing the money at the casino whereupon the dealers handled the bills.

BLISS BEHIND BARS

A prostitute in New York found herself on the wrong side of the law once too often, and ended up receiving a two-year sentence to be served in the women's penitentiary. Taking advantage of the courses and workshops on offer, she seemed to get on well with the other inmates and the months flew by. She was eventually released after serving 18 months and found a job in a department store. A couple of months later, the prison authorities were puzzled that a large number of women inmates at the penitentiary had become pregnant especially as most of them had been inside for over nine months. Investigating the matter, they also became puzzled by the fact that the former prostitute frequently came to visit the pregnant women and always brought presents. Delving into her past, they discovered a startling fact that solved their mystery – she was not in fact a female, but a very convincing male transvestite!

POLITE, BUT STUPID

A desperate man in England decided to rob a bank, so he went into a branch of Barclays and, like all polite bank robbers, joined the queue. In order to be a bit more discrete when making his demands, he took one of the counterfoils and wrote on it: "Dis iz a stikup. Poot all the mony in the bag." Then, worried that he might have been spotted writing the note, he panicked and left the bank. Spotting a branch of rival bank Lloyds across the road, he decided to try his luck there. Again, he joined the queue and eventually handed his note to the cashier. The cashier read the note and although alarmed, she realized from the bad spelling that the man probably wasn't very bright. She returned the note to him, saying sternly: "I'm afraid we can't accept this, sir, it's written on a Barclays Bank counterfoil." Unsure of himself, the man left Lloyds, returning to the branch of Barclays – where he was waiting patiently in the queue when the police, alerted by the Lloyds cashier, arrived to arrest him.

SPEEDING GHOSTS?

A highway-patrol police officer was close to signing himself into a mental institution after a series of freak readings on his speed detector. For several weeks he had been on the night shift, parking in his usual concealed spot off the main road. Several times he had just been drifting off to sleep to be suddenly woken up by his detector beeping wildly and displaying speeds of over 120 mph. Following in hot pursuit, however, the officer was mystified when he couldn't see any vehicles on the road at all. Communications with his colleague a few miles down the road revealed nothing further. After a few nights of high readings from seemingly invisible vehicles, he began to think he was losing his mind. The mystery was solved a few nights later though, when a car was found smashed by the side of the road. The dead driver was wearing infrared night-vision goggles and several kilos of cocaine were found in the panels of the car. The officer realized he wasn't mad after all and that his nightly apparitions were actually the drug-trafficker speeding by him with his lights off and using infrared goggles to see.

MODEL CITIZEN

A woman had just been to see Seven at a downtown cinema. As she returned to her car, she was approached by a man wearing a smart suit. He explained to her that he had noticed some dodgy-looking kids hanging around her car, so he had stayed around to keep an eye on it. He then asked if she could give him a lift because, as a result of guarding her car, he was now late for a business meeting. Although a bit jittery after the movie, the woman felt obliged to the man and agreed. When he got in the car, the woman noticed beads of sweat on his brow – and as it was a fairly cold day, she began to worry. She asked the man if he would get out and direct her out of the parking place. When he obliged, she sped off, leaving the man waving frantically behind her. Ten minutes later, having calmed down, she noticed that the man had left a briefcase on the floor of the car. Parking up, she opened the briefcase... and among some books and a few maps, she found a long knife with a serrated blade.

CAT BURGLAR

An elderly lady was heart-broken when her cat developed cancer and had to be put down. The woman told the nurse at the veterinary hospital that she would like to bury the cat in her garden and the nurse wrapped it in a box for the woman to carry home. On the way home, she passed a department store and decided to buy some flowers and a plaque to put on the cat's grave. She put the box by her and was telling the sales assistant what she wanted when she noticed that the box had disappeared. The sales assistant told security staff and they started to search the store for the box. It wasn't long before a security guard spotted the box in a telephone booth. The box had been opened and the dead cat was poking out of it. On the floor of the booth, a young boy was lying unconscious on the ground. It turned out that the boy was a well-known shoplifter. The boy must have taken the well-wrapped box, thinking it contained something valuable, and fainted when he glimpsed the dead cat.

THANK YOU LETTER

The Japanese are well known for their politeness but this example of gratitude is more mocking than respectful. Two weeks after the biggest bank robbery in Japan's history, the bank manager received a letter post-marked Rio de Janeiro, Brazil. The letter had been typewritten and read: "Thank you so much for the bonus. It may interest you to know that rather than the 50.5 million yen stated in newspapers, the amount was in fact 74.6 million yen." The criminals are presumably still living it up in South America.

PINCHER PINCHED

This story demonstrates that crime really doesn't pay. A young man was desperate to impress his girlfriend in the belief that impressing her would improve his chances of getting her into bed. One day, he came across a magazine article on aphrodisiac foods and decided that an elaborate meal might be the answer. He worked out a menu and went out to do some shoplifting. The oysters, asparagus and strawberries proved easy enough to steal, but lobster was proving to be a problem until the young man passed by a fish restaurant. Seeing a tank full of live lobsters, he entered the restaurant and when no one was looking, reached into the tank, pulled out a wriggling lobster and dropped it down his trousers. As he walked out of the restaurant, a sudden thought surfaced in the mind of the not-too-clever thief, but before he could act on it, he was doubled up on the floor, in agony. The lobster, in its panic, seized the nearest appendage with its large claw and as a result the thief was in no fit state to make his date that night. Indeed, he remained incapable of having sex for over five years and the wound never fully healed.

DOG'S DINNER

A couple returned to their residence in London, England after a night out at the theatre. Usually when they opened the front door, their Doberman, Bosley, would come bounding down the stairs and jump all over them, but this time… nothing. A little concerned, they looked round the house and eventually found Bosley lying in the corner, retching. The husband suspected that the dog had swallowed something that had become lodged in its throat but was unable to see anything. Using an emergency contact number, the man called a veterinarian who soon arrived and examined the dog. Having sedated the animal, he was able to remove the obstruction and everyone was shocked to see three bloody stumps that resembled human fingers. The police were called, searched the house and discovered a trail of blood leading down into the cellar. At the end of the trail they found a burglar, unconscious in a pool of blood, clutching his mutilated hand.

HOOKEY BUSINESS

A teenager out driving with his girlfriend pulled into a deserted car park, hoping to get lucky that night. He turned on the radio for some music and the couple got down to business. Things began to get steamy in the car, when the music suddenly stopped for a news flash. The newsreader reported that a homicidal maniac had escaped in the area, and warned people to look out for a man with a hook for a hand. When the music resumed, the boy tried to kiss the girl again, but she pushed him off and told him that she was scared and wanted to be taken home. The boy tried to argue with her, but realized that the moment had been ruined and gave in. Driving his girlfriend to her house, ever the gentlemen, he got out of the car to open her door. Arriving at her door, he was shocked to see a hook hanging off the handle.

ICY CURRENCY

A couple living in London, England consistently missed paying their electricity bill on time, and as a result were eventually forced by the power company to install a slot meter in their flat. As the woman was a specialist at making moulds, she made a set of moulds from a fifty pence piece – the coin used in the meter. By filling the moulds with water and placing them in the freezer, the couple found that within a few hours, they could make pieces of ice that would be accepted as valid coins by the meter. The plan worked successfully for a couple of months, but came to an end when a representative from the electricity company arrived to empty the meter only to find that it was full of water.

SMART THIEVES

This burglar must really have done his homework. A couple woke up to discover that their car had been stolen. They reported the robbery to the police, only to return from work the following day to find the car, cleaned and waxed, sitting in their driveway with an envelope on the driver's seat. A note inside the envelope apologized for taking the car. The writer explained that his mother had been taken seriously ill and he had had to take her to the hospital. With the note were two tickets to a concert that night. Surprised and delighted by this turn of events, the couple went to the concert where they enjoyed a very pleasant evening's entertainment. However, when they returned home, they discovered that their house had been thoroughly burgled and all their valuables had been stolen. A week later, the police informed them that their car had been used in a major bank robbery staged during the day it was missing.

TAKE TWO

A US congressman was interviewed live on the television news. The most central aspect of what he said was how successful the government had been in tackling crime. He was especially proud of the fact that violent street robberies were at an all-time low. On leaving the television station, the congressman went to his car parked outside. Suddenly, a man jumped out of the shadows and held him at gunpoint. The congressman lost his wallet, his watch and his car, but, best of all, the thief also stole his clothes. The humiliated congressman had to go back inside the television station completely naked, only to be spotted by the reporter who had just interviewed him. Five minutes later, the congressman gave a somewhat less confident interview.

DUMP IN A BANK

A bank robber was in the middle of holding up a bank, when the curry he'd eaten earlier started to make itself known. With the bank employees cowering on the floor, the robber demanded that the bank manager take him to the gents. The manager obliged and led him to a door behind the counter. The robber told everyone to stay where they were and, leaving the door slightly ajar, proceeded use the facilities. Scared that the robber could still see them, the employees didn't move. The robber eventually escaped with his loot but, to add insult to injury, he didn't flush the toilet and left an awful smell that lingered in the bank for days.

THE GREAT ESCAPE

A midget thief in Mexico was in the process of robbing a post office when he heard police sirens approaching. Realising he had been set up, the thief ran out of the back. The police stormed the building and the post office clerk told them where to find the thief. The Inspector smiled, "We have the place surrounded; he will not get away!" However, they looked all over the building, both inside and out, but they couldn't find the thief anywhere. The inspector sighed, clueless as to how the thief might have escaped, and went to use the post office toilet. As he undid his trousers, he noticed a huge mass of toilet paper in the toilet bowl, but thought nothing of it. He began to relieve himself, but he was startled to see the mass of toilet paper move. Staring up at him amongst the toilet paper was a pair of eyes. The inspector flushed the toilet and arrested the choking, besodden midget thief.

DEAD AND BURIED

A convicted bank robber, sentenced for life in Strangeways Prison, Manchester, came up with a plan to escape. He had noticed that when a prisoner dies, the body was placed in a coffin that was then nailed shut by the caretaker and transported to a local cemetery. The prisoner promised the caretaker a hefty slice of his buried loot if he helped him to escape. The caretaker agreed that he wouldn't nail the coffin shut until the morning and then after the funeral, he would dig him up. On the agreed night the prisoner, equipped with snacks and a flashlight, sneaked into the mortuary, squeezed into the coffin next to the dead body and managed to pull the lid over. With a few hours till the morning, the prisoner fell asleep. He awoke to hear the coffin being nailed shut and then felt the coffin being carried, put down and then transported. After about half an hour, the van stopped and the coffin was then carried and lowered into a grave. He could just about hear the priest's last rites and when that was over, he waited a few minutes more, before pulling out his flashlight and eating his snacks. Wondering how long it would be before the caretaker came to dig him up, curiosity got the better of him and he decided to have a look at who he was sharing the coffin with. He shone the flashlight on to the dead man's face, but was stunned to see that it was the caretaker himself.

A BAD TRIP

An Englishman gave in to temptation, while on a weekend break in Amsterdam, and bought a whole sheet of LSD to smuggle back into the UK. On the plane to Heathrow, however, the no-holds-barred message of the customs' adverts on drugs smuggling worried the man and, panicking, he consumed the whole sheet of acid. He passed through Customs unhindered, but just as he took a seat on the tube, the large dose of LSD struck. The man is now in a psychiatric unit convinced that he is a banana.

BAD PARKING

In New York a woman, returning to the car park from a shopping trip, spotted a man tampering with her BMW 740. She screamed at the man to go away, but he completely ignored her and opened the car door. The woman took a gun out of her handbag and told the man to go or she would shoot. The man responded by telling the woman that she was crazy and made to grab the gun, at which point the woman shot the man in the leg and got into the car. It was only when the woman's key didn't fit into the ignition, that she realised she had made a terrible mistake. Her BMW was on the other side of the car park.

JUST LIKE ON TV

The residents of a small town in Wiltshire were very excited, when a popular police TV show chose the area as a good place to film an episode. The film crew went round talking to residents and researching locations and had been in the town for two days when they visited a jewellery shop. The owner was not surprised when a young man with a clipboard came in and asked if they could film a scene in his shop. The owner, thinking it would be great for business, readily agreed and a few hours later, the young man returned with a video camera and three men wearing masks of various American presidents and carrying shotguns. The young man told the owner that he was going to film the men coming in, filling their bags full of jewels, then running out into a waiting car and driving off. All the owner had to do was look surprised and put his hands up. Everything went smoothly, the men filled their bags, ran out and the young man had followed them with the camera. However, when no-one had returned after 30 minutes, the owner realised he'd been duped and called the police.

GRANNY BUST

A grandmother from Hackney, babysitting for her daughter one night, got the scare of her life when half a dozen men burst into the flat, shouting and pointing submachine guns at her. It seems that the drug-busting brigade had misheard a communiqué from headquarters. They had been told to search the furthest flat on the left, not the first flat. Still, the police justified their over-the-top action when they found a few joints in the ashtray and a gram of skunk on the grandmother.

SWEET DREAMS

An American man, on trial for the murder of his wife, had the most unusual defence. He claimed he was sleep-walking and had no knowledge of his actions. However, when the jury heard the cases against him, they thought his game was up. His wife had been stabbed 40 times and when he was found he had even managed to bandage several cuts on his hands and dispose of his clothes. He had also been seen by several witnesses attempting to drown his wife in the swimming pool in the back garden. The man's lawyer calmly called to the stand an expert on sleep-walking. On hearing the evidence, the expert stated simply that this was all possible while sleep-walking. The courts can expect a surge in cases of crimes committed while sleep-walking.

POISON PEN LETTERS

A man, who had been sentenced to four months community service in Washington, DC, managed to extend his sentence to 12 years imprisonment. The man, convicted of simple embezzlement, drew the authority's wrath after writing letter after letter to several presidents, judges and congressmen. Nothing wrong with that you might say, but each letter attacked the recipient's sexuality and sometimes even resorted to death threats. The man was then refused access to pen and paper, and was told to spend his remaining time in reading.

PIMPLY PIMP

A 13-year-old boy was convicted of attempting to organise a prostitution ring in a small town in Louisiana. The boy, far from defending himself, bragged about how he had convinced girls in his class to work for him. Several boys in his school had each paid between $5 to $15 for intimate encounters with his "employees", although there was no evidence that sex occurred. The 13-year-old pimp told the court he had so far made $95 out of the "business", which he had already spent on a trendy pair of trainers.

CRIME DOESN'T PAY

A boy from San Francisco, fresh out of school, had just landed a job as a department store detective. Full of enthusiasm, he was eager to catch as many shoplifters as he could. One summer's day, he saw a suspicious-looking man wandering around. The man had been in the store for over an hour, picking up items, looking around and putting them back again. The young detective watched as the man eventually approached the cash till with a children's colouring book. As the man handed a $10 note to the cashier, he leaned over, grabbed the cash-till tray and ran out of the store. The detective was about to give chase when the cashier shouted to him not to bother. Waving the $10 note at the detective, the cashier smiled and said, "There was only $2.15 in the till. We made a profit!"

THE NIGHT BUST

Three students, who shared a flat in Manchester, went on a pub crawl one Friday night, only to get completely inebriated and miss the last bus home. Cheapskate students that they were, they began to walk the few miles home. However, on passing the bus depot, the students had an idea and sneaked inside. They found their bus, the 157, parked by the gate and so started her up and drove themselves home, leaving the bus at the nearest bus stop. Delighting in their new-found free transport home, they repeated the exercise the next weekend. The weekend after that, they tried again, but this time they took their time and the police caught them. The police confirmed that the students' fingerprints matched those found in the previous week's thefts. Asked why they took so long this time, one student replied sadly, "The bus company must've been on to us, because they'd parked the 157 right at the back and we had to move five other buses to get it out!"

RATS

A judge in Bombay, India, was forced to dismiss a case against a man accused of murdering and robbing a market trader. The man had been caught red-handed with the bag of wheat he had allegedly snatched from the trader after allegedly hitting him over the head with a rock. The man was arrested and the bag of wheat taken as evidence. However, when the case came to court, rats had completely destroyed the bag of wheat and, with no witnesses of the event, the judge dismissed the case due to lack of evidence.

CHIPS AND MAYONNAISE

A Belgian man held up a corner shop with a gun, shouting at customers to lie down on the floor with their hands over their heads. As he went from one customer to another, emptying their pockets and taking their valuables, he came across one woman who had been eating chips and mayonnaise at the time. Unable to resist the intoxicating smell, the man grabbed a handful of chips and stuffed them into his mouth. Satisfied with his ill-gotten gains, the man went to leave. However, as he did so, he slipped on a chip that he had dropped and knocked himself out. An arresting police officer commented, "Many a robber has been caught because they succumbed to the temptation of our celebrated chip."

CURRIED BURGLAR

In Birmingham, a professional burglar's career was cut short when he picked the house of a chutney enthusiast. Trouble started when he broke in through the kitchen window and promptly fell headfirst into a very large jar of home-made mango chutney. Unable to remove the jar, the man tried to smash it against the wall, but was overcome by the chutney's potent fumes. The home-owner returned from his night out to find the burglar unconscious on the kitchen floor. He later told police, "He might not have survived if he'd landed in my lime pickle."

DIY BURGLARS

A recent spate of burglaries in Sydney, Australia, had bemused police and shown a more altruistic approach to the crime. A man came back from a weekend break to find that his house had been broken into and his tv and video stolen, but the burglars had completely redecorated the house. The man told police he was delighted with their choice of colour scheme and their work was worth his tv and video. Another woman came back from a two-week holiday to find burglars had renovated her garden and added a pond in return for a set of silver candlesticks - "Better than any landscape gardening I've seen," quipped the woman. Detectives are offering up their houses to catch the burglars after finding out that some burglaries have involved improving the feng shui of residences.

TO CATCH A FLASHER

In Pretoria, South Africa, an old man was known for his habit of flashing at women in cars at red lights, but had somehow evaded arrest. One day, however, he opened his overcoat on an innocent woman driver only for her to instantly react by closing her electric window on the old man's pecker. To the delight of passers-by, the woman slowly drove the offensive man to the nearest police station and had him arrested.

CURSING, SNEEZING WASHING MACHINE

A rich old lady had a washing machine delivered to her house after her old one broke down. Over the next few hours, she kept hearing someone sneezing and muttering, but when she turned around there was no-one there. She really thought she was going mad when she used her washing machine for the first time. During the spin cycle the washing machine uttered some very abusive profanities. A superstitious person, the old lady asked her local priest to exorcise the machine, but to no avail. Finally, she called an engineer, who took the washing machine apart to find a midget trapped beneath the drum. Apparently, the midget had hoped to emerge from the washing machine and rob the old lady's house, but he had got wedged inside.

STUCK FAST

Two prisoners managed to escape from a high security prison in Tunisia by using Superglue. When their jailer came to close their cell door, the prisoners grabbed a hand each. At first, the jailer expected them to overpower him and escape, but when he tried to shake free of them, he discovered they had glued themselves to him. Attempts to remove the prisoners with alcohol proved fruitless and the three of them were taken to the local hospital for surgical removal. As soon as the surgeon had performed the task, however, the prisoners escaped. All arts and crafts activities have since been banned inside the prison.

HEAVY WEIGHT

This story might shine some light on why most truck drivers are so big. A 20-stone truck driver from Barcelona, Spain, was delivering a load to Marseilles, France, when he spotted a man on the side of the road waving frantically. Obviously thinking the man's car had broken down, the truck driver pulled up. As the truck driver went to get out, however, the man ran up to him and, pointing a gun, demanded that the truck driver get out. When the truck driver took his time, the impatient man pulled on his arm, only to pull too hard. The 20-stone driver fell right on top of the man, breaking both his arms and causing several other unpleasant injuries. Since the event the driver has gained another four stone just in case he comes across a more resilient road bandit in the future.

STUCK FAST II

In Melbourne, Australia, another prisoner put Superglue to the test in a bid for freedom. The said prisoner liberally doused his overalls in Superglue and stuck himself to the side of the laundry van as it left the prison. A few miles down the road, the van stopped at a red light and the prisoner saw his opportunity. However, when he tried unzipping himself from the overalls as planned, he found that the zip had stuck fast and no amount of squirming or wriggling helped. Four hours later, the prisoner was apprehended when the laundry van returned to the prison with clean linen.

PLAN NOSE-DIVES

A Brazilian man, desperate for money, decided to rob a bank. Unable to find a real gun, he used an imitation pistol. He planned to threaten the cashier with the fake gun, take the money and leave taking a customer with him as a hostage. Like most plans, it failed as soon as it began. The man entered the bank, queued in line and when it was his turn, brandished the gun and told the cashier to hand him all the money. However, the man's nose, which was particularly large, made the cashier laugh. A little embarrassed, the man was determined to keep his authority, so in his most assertive voice demanded that she hand him the money, but this just made her laugh all the harder. Pretty soon, the whole bank was in hysterics and as a result the poor man ran out in tears.

DISJOINTED

A police officer was lecturing children on the dangers of drugs in a community centre in Moss Side, Manchester. The officer took out a real cannabis joint and passed it round on a dish, so that the children could see and smell it. He warned the children not to remove it, pointing out that he had to take the joint back to the evidence room, and if it was not there when the dish came back, he would have to search them all. However, when the dish returned, the officer was surprised to see that not only was the joint still there, but that it had been joined by two more joints, three wraps of speed and a rock of crack.

UNHITCHED

A lawyer was driving to his home in Guildford from a conference in Swansea. He spotted a hitchhiker by the side of the road and, feeling like some company, stopped and picks the man up. A few miles down the road, the lawyer began to worry. The hitchhiker had an evil look to him and talked in a menacing voice. The lawyer then realised that he would be completely unprepared if the hitchhiker were to threaten him, so he was relieved when he spotted another hitchhiker. He stopped to pick up the second man, who was wearing a suit and appears very friendly. However, not long after driving off, the second hitchhiker produced a knife and told the lawyer to pull over and get out. Somehow, as everybody got out of the car, the first hitchhiker managed to grab the knife off the second one and knocked him out. The first hitchhiker, gruffly remarking "Amateur", took the unconscious man's wallet and offered half the contents to the aghast lawyer, who refused the money. Reading the lawyer's thoughts, the hitchhiker explained that it was his day off and he was just visiting his mother in London.

THE SUNDAY BANK ROBBER

A not-too-clever man from Birmingham, England, wanted to rob a bank but, as it was a Sunday, he opted to rob a bank's automatic teller machine instead. The man scribbled a note which said, "Give me all your money or I'll blow you sky-high," and fed the piece of paper into the appropriate slot. After three tries without result, the man started smashing the machine with a hammer when a police patrol spotted and arrested the foolish man.

THE MISSING HUSBAND

In a small town in Louisiana, a woman reported to the police that she was extremely worried because her husband had not returned home one night. The police made some enquiries and when, after a few days, the husband had still not shown up, they set up a search party. An extensive search of the area proved fruitless and, after a week, the case was left unsolved. A week later, however, the local water authority received an influx of reports from residents complaining that their tap water had an extremely foul odour and taste to it. The water authority investigated the complaints and traced the problem to a water tower on the outskirts of town. On draining the water tower, they discovered a body that had been weighed down with rocks. The body was identified as the woman's husband.

CLEAN PICTURES

An old man from Derby, England, took a roll of a film into a chemists to be developed. The next day, the man returned to pick up his photos, only to be greeted by several policemen and arrested. The chemist had reported the man to the police after discovering that the film contained photos of little children in the nude. It turned out the chemist had jumped to the wrong conclusion, however, when it was found that the children in the photos were the man's grandchildren, who, without the man's knowledge, had taken the camera and photographed each other in the bath.

THE ABDUCTED BABY

An English couple and their baby were on holiday in Turkey and were wandering around a busy market. At one point, both the mother and the father were distracted by a loud argument between two people and when they turned back to their baby, she had been replaced by a large watermelon. The distraught couple went straight to the police, but further investigation proved fruitless. A few days later, a policeman on the Turkish-Greek border stopped a couple travelling through, but became suspicious when he noticed that the baby the woman was carrying was very pale. Further examination revealed that the baby was dead and its body was stuffed with heroin. It was, of course, the English couple's abducted baby.

THE NEW YORK MUGGER

A man from New York was walking down the street when he discovered his wallet was missing just after being bumped by a passer-by. The man, thinking he had been pick-pocketed, ran back and spotted the man who bumped him. Furious, he took the man down a side street, beat him up and, believing that the man must have ditched his wallet and taken out the money, took all the cash that the man had on him. However, when the man returned home he found his wallet on the kitchen table where he must have left it that morning.

THE BLEEDING MAN

In Prague, Czechoslovakia, a man boarded an underground train with blood dripping from his jacket pocket. Other passengers, obviously thinking the man had been injured, offered to help him, but the man just ignored them. At the next station, two policemen boarded the train and an old woman, thinking she was being helpful, pointed out the blood on the man. The policemen detained the man for questioning and eventually discovered that the man was hiding a woman's cut-off finger with a diamond ring attached to it. The man tried to explain that he had found the finger while walking in the park, but the policemen were unconvinced and arrested him.

THE SWITCH

In Buenos Aires, Argentina, a woman, in a hurry to get to a dentist's appointment, decided to risk a shortcut through a park known for its criminal element. Suddenly, the woman felt her necklace being snapped off and, before the attacker could run off, she turned round sharply, grabbed his neck chain and snapped that off. Both ran away in opposite directions. When safely out of the park the woman examined the neck chain and, impressed by the look of it, took it to a jeweller. The woman was delighted by the exchange - her necklace had just been a gold-plated fake, the neck chain was 22-carat gold.

THE COWBOY DEALER

A blackjack dealer in a casino in Atlanta, Georgia, had the habit of wearing cowboy boots. One time when he was raking in the gamblers' silver dollars, one of the dollars accidentally slipped off the table and down into his boot without anyone seeming to notice. The dealer decided that this was a good way to make some extra money and he began to collect at least $20 a night using this method, until, stupidly, he got greedy and began shoving more and more dollars down. One night he got so carried away that, when it came to the end of his shift and he tried to take a step, he couldn't move because of the weight of all the silver dollars in his boot. With everyone around watching, the dealer heaved as hard as he could, but eventually fell over. Silver dollars spilled out all over the place and the dealer was sacked.

ROOM WITH A SMELL

A couple on holiday in Bangkok, Thailand, checked into a fancy hotel in the centre of the city. When they entered their room, they noticed a terrible smell and unable to see where it could be coming from, they called the reception desk, who sent up a maid. The maid looked around but found nothing, so she sprayed the room with air freshener and left. However, the smell still lingered, so the couple took it upon themselves to investigate. Eventually, they decided that the smell was emanating from the bed. The man lifted up the mattress and there pressed against the bed frame was the decomposing body of what turned out to be a prostitute.

THE DEMO

A couple of ambitious youths broke into an exclusive recording studio in Oxford, England, to try and make a demo of a song they had written. On the third take of their song, they spotted a police car driving up the driveway so, quick as a flash, they turned out all the lights and hid inside a cupboard. The policemen had come to investigate after neighbours reported some suspicious characters loitering at the entrance earlier. As they approached the studio room, they heard two voices whispering. At first puzzled where the voices were coming from, they soon realised they were coming from the speakers. One of the boys had unwittingly taken the microphone inside with him. The police were amused to hear one boy cursing the other for standing on his toe, before one of them revealed their whereabouts with "They'll never find us in this cupboard."

EAGLE EYES

In Vancouver, Canada, a burglar broke into a house and had filled his bag with lots of loot, when he suddenly felt a pair of eyes on him. Looking up, he saw an eagle staring right at him with cold, merciless eyes. Initially the man was too petrified to move but after ten minutes he tried creeping towards the door, however the eyes just followed him, so he stayed rooted to the spot. Eventually, the homeowners turned up and found the thief motionless in their lounge. Once the homeowner had turned on the light, the thief could see that the eagle was stuffed, but it was too late and the man was arrested. The homeowner commented, "That stuffed eagle was better than any watchdog, I can tell you."

AN APPETITE FOR LITERATURE

An English boy studying for his school exams got into the habit of nibbling bits of paper while revising. He became so engrossed in this habit that he began to consume whole pages and before long whole books. His habit turned to obsession and, as an English Literature student, he started choosing which books to eat. He found that the pages of Shakespearian plays were much tastier than Thomas Hardy novels and ate his way through all his works from "Hamlet" to "Cymbeline". However, when he discovered that the older the edition the better the taste, he soon landed himself in trouble. One day, the police were called into a rare books shop when the owner discovered the hapless boy nibbling on a first edition copy of "Macbeth". The boy is now in a psychiatric institution where they are trying to wean him off Shakespeare and on to modern poetry, such as Philip Larkin, in a vain hope that he will soon tire of the habit.

NOT HIS LUCKY DAY

In Madrid, Spain, a man went to drown his sorrows in a local bar after a disastrous day - he had lost his job, his wife had left him and his gambling debts were being called in by the local Mafioso. The man got so drunk that on the way home, he broke into a house via the back garden and filled a suitcase full of valuables. To cover any trace of the crime, the inebriated man set fire to the curtains and left the same way he had come in. However, on turning the corner to his road, dragging the heavily-laden suitcase behind, he was shocked to see fire engines arriving outside his house. In his drunken state, the man had burgled and burnt down his own house!

THE SIPHONING TRICK

A man travelling around Australia ran out of petrol in the middle of nowhere. It was late at night and there were no petrol stations marked on his map for miles. However, he noticed on his map that a few miles down the road there was a campsite. Hoping to find petrol there, he took a petrol can and walked to the campsite. He got there and was delighted to see that there were some campervans parked there. However, there were no signs of life and the man didn't want to wake anybody up at this late hour. The man decided his only option was to try to siphon out petrol from one of the campervans. He got a tube, opened the tank and, as quietly as possible, he began sucking out the contents. He expected the petrol to taste nasty but the stuff he was siphoning out was really foul. It was only when he spat it out that he realised he had opened the campervan's toilet holding tank by mistake. After vomiting up the entire contents of his stomach, the man decided to leave it until the morning and returned to his car to try and get some sleep.

THE LIE DETECTOR

In Sao Paulo, Brazil, police used a colander and a photocopying machine to trick a dim-witted robber into confessing to a crime. Convinced of his guilt but lacking sufficient evidence to convict the man, the police placed a colander on the man's head, attached wires from it to a photocopying machine and told the robber that it was a lie detector. If the police suspected that the robber was not telling the truth, the sergeant would press a button on the photocopier and a sheet of paper would come out with "Lie" printed on it. If they thought he was telling the truth, the sergeant would quickly change the sheet of paper with one that said "True". After several questions, the robber, convinced that the machine was indeed a lie detector, signed a confession to a series of crimes, including some that the policemen had been unaware of.

AN INCONVENIENCE

In Bucharest, Romania, police were quite concerned about a spate of thefts from public toilets. They had had several reports from embarrassed gentlemen, who said that while they were using the lavatories, they suddenly saw a pair of hands dart under the door and grab their feet. The mysterious assailant would then make off with their shoes. Surveillance of various public toilets failed to catch the thief, so a policeman was sent undercover. The policeman caught a number of drug dealers and sex offenders before finally nabbing the shoe thief by wearing a pair of 18-hole army boots. The unfortunate thief took so long trying to untie the laces that the policeman had quietly radioed for backup and had him arrested.

DEAD-END JOB

A woman was charged with harbouring a dead body, when she made her husband continue working after he died of a heart attack. The woman, who ran a bar in Nairobi, Kenya, discovered her husband had died of a heart attack after she came back from a shopping trip. Worried that without her husband customers would stop coming to their bar, she propped him up in a rocking chair in the corner and told any concerned customers that he was just tired. The woman got away with it for nearly two weeks until one customer got suspicious when her husband wouldn't join in a conversation about football. As police led her away, the woman was heard to say, "He's not dead. His heart just stopped beating, that's all."

ACTION BOY

In Sarajevo, an eight-year-old boy was convicted of armed bank robbery. The boy took to crime after his mother refused to buy him an Action Man. Bitter and twisted, the boy took his father's shotgun and went straight to the city bank and ordered the cashier to give him the equivalent of $100, so that he could buy the whole collection of Action Men. Thinking it was a joke, the cashier laughed and told him not to be so silly and to go home before his mother began to worry. However, after the boy fired the gun into the ceiling, the cashier took him seriously and quickly handed him the money. Soon after, the police caught the boy at the toy shop, trying to decide which Action Men he wanted as he had underestimated the cost of the whole collection.

WHAT A GAS!

A man, who lived in Hong Kong, was convicted of manslaughter after a failed suicide went horribly wrong. Following several other failed attempts, the man put his head in an oven and tried to gas himself. Unfortunately, a concerned neighbour popped round with a lit cigarette, causing a huge explosion which destroyed the whole apartment block and killed nine people. Miraculously, the man survived with minor burns, apparently because the oven shielded him from the collapsing building.

WHAT A TRIP

A student at a remote rural college liked nothing better than to play dangerously and take LSD. Such was his capacity that, come one birthday, he decided to treat himself to four trips in one session. While staggering about the campus he suddenly thought it would be a good idea to climb a tree, which he promptly fell out of, breaking his arm. He was rushed to hospital and, while nobody guessed the illegal truth behind his fall, he was still hallucinating wildly as he went under anaesthetic. At least, he reasoned with what was left of his reason, he'd be okay when he awoke. Some time later he came out of his slumber. The police had not been called, he was safe but, the unfortunate hippy realized to his horror, he was still tripping away.

WASTED

A young teacher and her friends were enjoying a particularly noisy evening at home getting drunk and generally annoying the neighbours in a quiet and painfully dull London suburb. Despite repeated requests to keep the noise down, the household took no notice and carried on partying into the night. When the drink began to run out one person was nominated to go out and get some more beers while the rest remained behind in order to study the effects of marijuana on the under 30s. No sooner had that person left than there was a knock at the door. Assuming that the beer-getter had forgotten the money, one of the party animals went to answer the door, having first taken the trouble to put a wastepaper basket on his head. "Come on in you silly sod," he shouted and led his friend back into the living room just moments after the female teacher had been handed the only joint in the room that was still burning. Unfortunately for all concerned, the party animal with the bin on his head had, in fact, led the police into the living room, where they conveyed the neighbours' concerns about the noise before leading the poor teacher off to the police station to receive a caution.

HEAVY METAL

Police in Auckland were deeply alarmed to discover that someone had broken into the National Radiation Laboratory and stolen a container of radioactive material that just happened to be lying around. The radioactive material was – and still is – lethal, and at first, police were concerned that the break-in might have been the work of terrorists. They took a different view, however, when they were informed that the radioactive material was being stored in a lead container weighing over 500 pounds. From that moment on they went searching the local scrap yards trying to find someone who had brought in a large quantity of dodgy lead, but to no avail. Eventually, they received a phone call from the mother of a couple of small boys who said that she had found her sons trying to make lead weights for fishing from a large block that had been dumped in her garden at some time in the night.

BAG OF SHITE

When someone says that the shit hit the fan, they are not usually talking about a rapid interaction between turd and twirly thing. For the occupants of a court in Sri Lanka, however, the term for once was very close to the truth. During the trial of a man accused of the disappointingly mundane crime of stealing gas pipes from his employer, the accused kept trying to draw the judge's attention to the brutal treatment he had received at the hands of the police. As is usually the case in these situations, the judge refused to believe that the police were capable of such things. Having failed to get the judge to take him seriously, the defendant pulled out a turd-filled plastic bag and attempted to throw it at a group of police officers who were sitting in the court. Unfortunately, he missed. The resulting shit hitting the fan incident showered the entire court in inadmissible evidence and the case had to be delayed. The defendant was later charged with insulting the dignity of the court.

WELL HIDDEN

Police in California were baffled by the disappearance of a thief who ran out of the back door of a shop he had just robbed just as officers of the law charged in through the front door. The rear of the shop opened out on to a deserted, high-walled alleyway, and the street to which the alleyway led was also deserted. They searched for the robber for over an hour but were unable to find him. For the next five days the officers involved in the incident puzzled over where the man could have gone. There were no obvious hiding places and so it seemed that the man had simply disappeared into thin air. Eventually the man's whereabouts became known to the police after they heard banging coming from the boot of their patrol car. The officers pulled over and opened the boot to investigate the noise and discovered, to their great surprise, the thief, who had been hiding in there afraid to come out for the previous five days.

SNOOKER

Police in the fishing town of Grimsby in the north of England were puzzled by the number of car thefts reported on one single day. While there is nothing unusual about car theft, the number of cars involved - especially the number of red cars involved - gave them cause for concern. The police decided to set a trap in order to catch the thieves and, to this end, left a red car apparently unlocked and unattended in a car park known to be popular with car thieves. They went off to lie in wait and hadn't been waiting long before someone took the bait and attempted to drive the car away. The police grabbed the villain and tried to find out from him what had been going on. It emerged that the reason so many cars, and especially red cars, were being stolen that day was that rival gangs were indulging in a game of "snooker". This involved them stealing a red car, then picking a colour from the set of snooker balls before stealing another red car - and so on until they finished off 'potting' a black car.

FINGERED

When a thief broke into a house in the middle of the night, he disturbed its occupants by smashing a window as he climbed in. Soon lights began to come on and he heard the noises of the householders upstairs. In his rush to escape, he left rather more than a few fingerprints behind. As he climbed back out though the broken window, he managed to slice his finger off, leaving it behind as evidence. After the police arrived they put out an appeal on local radio, requesting that the burglar go to the local hospital where surgeons were waiting to sew his finger back on. Faced with the prospect of a short prison term or the rest of his life being deficient in the digit department, the man had little choice but to turn up at the hospital and get stitched up in every respect.

HAPPY SNAPS

An old lady had entered a photo booth to get a picture for Senior Citizens' Pass and was just about to pull her best toothless grin when a callow youth stuck his head into the booth and attempted to steal her hand bag. As he got a grip on the handle, so too did she and in the resulting struggle the little thug was pulled into the booth. At that very moment the first of four pictures was taken and the resulting flash startled them both for a second. Quickly coming to her senses, the old lady resumed pulling on the bag and once again the youth was pulled into the booth. Again there was a flash, but this time the young man realized that he had met his match and made a break for it, with the old lady in tow. Tracking down the would-be thief was easy of course, as the police had his picture, and evidence of his crime, from the old lady's attempts to get a photograph for her travel card.

HEADBANGER

A young couple drove into the grounds of a mental institution and parked up with a view to looking at the stars and listening to the radio. While they were sitting there a report came over the airwaves warning that a dangerous patient has escaped from the very institution in the grounds of which they were parked. Deciding not to take any chances, the couple attempted to start the car and drive to somewhere safer. Unfortunately, the car would not start and so the man decided to go and get help, telling his girlfriend to lock the car door behind him and not to get out for any reason. After a while, she saw a blue flashing light in the distance and, at the same time, heard a loud banging noise from the roof of the car. The police car pulled up and an officer told the girl to get out of the car but not to look at the roof of her vehicle. Of course, she looked. There on the roof of the car sat a man with mad staring eyes and her boyfriend's head in his hands.

DENTAL HYGENE

No book of urban myths would be complete without this one. A family returned from their holidays to find that their house had been burgled and all of their possessions, bar the toothbrushes and a camera, had been taken. The family informed the police, filed the usual insurance claims and then went about their business, thinking nothing of using the toothbrushes. A couple of days later they took their holiday photographs to be developed, along with the film that was in the one remaining camera. When the prints were returned they discovered that the film from the camera featured photographs of their toothbrushes, stuffed up the backsides of the burglars.

MEDICAL

It is inevitable that myths will arise around the medical profession. More than in any other area of our lives, we are forced to take on trust almost everything a doctor tells us. Few people, when all is said and done, have the knowledge or resources to do anything other than this. Because we are pushed into this position, our worst fears run through our minds and, before too long, we become more than willing to believe almost anything we hear about activities in a hospital or in the doctor's consulting room. There can, after all, be very few people who have not heard rumours about patients going into hospital for minor operations, only to wake up and find that they have lost an arm or a leg – or worse. These myths feed our fears and yet, in a strange way, provide comfort when we need it most.

It is reassuring to get to a hospital and find that the person who is to carry out our operation is not a deranged mad man, but a perfectly ordinary human being. A human being who is just as concerned to get the operation right as we are for him or her to get it right.

Read the following tales and enjoy them, if for no other reason than it wasn't you on the operating table.

FLASHBACK

A medical student in London had his final exams coming up, so he decided to have some dangerous fun before settling down to revising for them. He went out to a party and proceeded to take some LSD and have a mind-expanding experience. After recovering from the weekend, he got down to some work and the next week went to take his first exam. When the exam was over, the student felt confident he had answered the questions impressively. When the professor picked up his paper and scanned it, he suddenly said, "What's this? Where are your answers? The confused student looked at the paper and realised what had happened. The student had answered each question splendidly, but experiencing a flashback to the LSD, he had squeezed each answer into one tiny line!

FRIGHTENING JOKE

Medical students sometimes have a strange sense of humour, as this tale from a medical school in London, England reveals. Following a compulsory class on the dissection of a human corpse, a group of students decided to have a bit of fun. When no-one was looking, they removed the corpse's penis, placed it in a plastic bag and took it away. That night, at the university's student bar, they planned their little practical joke. They went down to the male toilets and waited for other drunken students to come in to relieve themselves. When a likely candidate came in, one of them went to a urinal and pretended to take a leak. Suddenly, the prankster began screaming as if he were in agony and began brandishing the dead man's penis. The medical students took turns to perform the trick during the course of the evening and as a result, it is understood several male students began to handle their penises with great care when using the toilet...

DOUBLE DAMAGE

One night, an ambulance was sent to pick up a man, reported to be in need of medical attention, from the side of a road. The ambulance driver drove down the road slowly, looking for the man on the verge. Suddenly, there was a bump as the ambulance appeared to run over something. In an attempt to work out what it was, the driver reversed back, only to run over the same thing again. It slowly dawned on the ambulance driver what he had just done – twice. Back at the hospital, doctors were mystified why a man coming in with a bad heart condition had two broken legs.

TWINKLE, TWINKLE LITTLE...

An American woman was on holiday visiting a friend. After a night out on the town she ended up sleeping with a guy, and a few days later developed a curious rash around her genitals. Concerned, her girlfriend recommended that she visit her gynecologist. As any woman might feel on being seen by a friend's gynecologist, she wanted to smell as fresh as possible, so she used her friend's deodorant spray. She arrived at the surgery and somewhat nervously waited to be seen. Eventually, the gynecologist called her name and she entered his consulting room. She followed the doctor's instructions to put on a gown and lie on the examination table, and he began to examine her. Almost immediately he looked up and said: "Wow, we are flashy. Have you got something special on tonight?" Completely embarrassed and very puzzled, the woman looked down and, seeing lots of sparkly stuff, she realized that she had mistaken her friend's glitter hairspray for vaginal deodorant.

TASTY CLUES

A lecturer at a medical school was trying to convey the importance of using the sense of taste during the process of diagnosis. To demonstrate his point he conducted a diabetes test. The lecturer asked some of his students to provide urine samples for the test. When the students brought back the flasks of their urine, the lecturer dipped a finger into a sample and then licked it, telling his students that he could determine the sugar content by the taste. He then told the students to repeat the tests themselves. Although most of them were feeling a bit ill from the suggestion, they all feared failure if they refused to go along with the request. After the students performed the test, albeit with looks of disgust on their faces, the lecturer moved on to reveal the importance of observation in diagnosis. He showed them that he had been dipping his index finger in the urine samples before licking his middle finger. At which point, several students ran to the classroom windows and were violently sick.

MICROSCOPIC EVIDENCE

A teacher told his biology class about the common types of bacteria found in saliva. Frustrated by his students' apparent lack of interest, he told them they were about to undertake an experiment. After showing them pictures of what they could expect to find, he asked the students to take scrapings from inside their mouths and view them under the microscope. A female student examined her sample, but was unable to identify a particular type of cell, so she asked the teacher to have a look. He took a look through her microscope and then exclaimed: "Well, I never, that's a human sperm cell". Immediately, a male student who everyone knew as the girl's long-term boyfriend, shouted at the girl: "You bitch, you've never given me a blow job!" The girl broke down in tears and ran out of the room.

OUT OF THE CLOSET

In another biology class, the teacher was lecturing about the human reproductive system. At one point, she mentioned that fructose, a complex sugar, is a major component of sperm. On hearing this, a puzzled student raised his hand and innocently asked: "Why does sperm taste so salty then?" All the other students burst out laughing. Realizing the implication of what he has said, the young man addressed the class: "Well, I was going to come out soon anyway. Hey, everybody, I'm gay and I'm proud." Satisfied with the effect of his proclamation, he stood up and walked out, leaving everybody gaping.

DELAYED REACTION

A woman who had lost control of her bowel movements was diagnosed as having a rare condition. Fortunately, technology had an answer and a device was surgically implanted in her backside. In order to go to the toilet all she had to do was pass a magnet over a sensor in her abdomen to open her bowels. The device worked superbly and the woman began to enjoy a new lease of life. In fact, she was so delighted with the freedom the device gave her, that she quit her job and decided to travel around the world for a year. As she boarded the first of her flights and settled in her seat, she realized that she might have made a mistake – the airport security X-ray machine had triggered off the device, delivering an unpleasant mess into her pants.

SUCKED HIS NUTS...

An old man was in hospital recovering from a major operation. A christian boy had volunteered to visit patients who didn't get many visitors. The old man was one such patient and the lad visited him three times a week and enjoyed their chats. The old man would always have some sweets to offer the young lad. One week, the old man was due to be discharged and on the eve of his departure, the lad came and sat down next to him. The old man was so excited at the prospect of going home that he'd forgotten to provide any sweets. He did have a bag of peanuts though and, somewhat embarrassed, he offered them to the lad. The lad listened to the old man talking about what he'd do when he got back home and munched on the peanuts. When it was time for the lad to go, the old man, seeing that he'd finished the bag of peanuts, remarked how hungry he must be and added: "I don't actually like peanuts, so I just suck the chocolate off them."

TOO CLEVER BY HALF

A hospital surgeon was out on his stag night on the eve of his wedding. It was the usual drunken mayhem and the groom drank so much that he blacked out. As a prank, his medical friends carried him to the hospital and put his left leg in a cast. The next morning, he woke up in bed, still a little woozy, and went into a panic about his leg.

His best man told him he was lucky to have escaped from his fall with only a simple fracture of the left leg. The groom was forced to get married on crutches and even spent the reception in plaster. As the couple were driven off to the honeymoon, the groom's friends decided that they should tell him the truth. They phoned the hotel where the newlyweds were staying and left a message that his leg was not in fact broken. Unfortunately, in order to prevent his friends interfering with his honeymoon, the groom had given them the number of a different hotel.

BABY PUNK

Back in the Seventies, a young punk woman was in the maternity wing of St Thomas's Hospital in south London. When it was time, the pink-mohicaned anarchist was taken into the delivery room and attended to by a midwife and a doctor. The woman was screaming in pain and the midwife told her to calm down while the doctor had a look. The doctor was mildly amused to see that the woman had died her pubic triangle green. He also noticed that she had a tattoo just above, but because of her pregnant state the writing was all distorted. Curious and trying to make small talk to calm her down, the doctor asked her what it said. The woman stopped screaming, stared at him and then said gruffly, "It says 'Keep off the grass', dunnit?" Soon after, the woman gave birth to a healthy, pink baby boy.

EARLY MORNING AROUSAL

A researcher from the Health Education Authority became curious about a small town in the Lake District of northern England, after coming across an alarmingly large increase in the number of births being reported. Eager to investigate this phenomenon, the researcher decided to spend a weekend in the town. The researcher stayed in a friendly bed and breakfast, but after a day scrutinizing the town's records, still couldn't understand what could be causing the residents to have so many children. At about 6am on Monday morning, the researcher was suddenly woken by a loud rumbling and he felt like the whole building was shaking. Worried that it might be an earthquake, the researcher ran downstairs and banged on the landlady's door. The landlady eventually managed to calm him down and told him that the rumbling was due to a freight train that passed by every weekday morning at about the same time. The landlady went on to explain that the town had been a victim to the train's rumblings since the tracks were strengthened over a year ago. The researcher, understanding the effects on couples being woken up early in the morning, realized what was causing the mysterious population explosion.

DEAR JOHN

Medical students in their final year at Harvard University had been dreading the practical autopsy exam, but, on the day, they all crowded into the examination room to find their professor standing next to what was obviously a cadaver under a sheet. After everyone had settled down, the professor gleefully announced, "We're extremely lucky today. We have been able to secure a young fresh male cadaver from New York, who tragically took his own life yesterday." As the professor removed the sheet, a young female student suddenly fainted. It turned out that the body was that of the boyfriend she had dumped only a few days previously.

ARMLESS FUN

A group of medical students at Bristol University hit upon a novel prank they could play. They managed to get hold of an arm of a cadaver and then drove off towards the Severn Bridge. Just before they reached the toll booth over the bridge, the driver put the dead arm through the sleeve of his jacket and placed several coins in its hand. The student drove up to the toll booth and extended the arm. The poor man behind the toll booth must have been horrified when the car drove off, leaving him holding the limb. Unfortunately for the students, however, fingerprints were taken from the hand of the arm, traced back to the cadaver at the university and the group of students identified. The students were not expelled, but their professor failed them in anatomy because it seemed they had used a left arm instead of a right arm.

UNARMED

In American in the Fifties medical students at a well-known university were irritated that a woman had been allowed to enrol on the course, and several of them decided to frighten her away. One night, they left a pickled arm from a cadaver in the woman's bed, hoping that she would see the arm, realize that she wasn't cut out for a medical profession and drop out. However, the students didn't bank on her reacting as badly as she did.

The woman had been out drinking that night and so when she retired, she mistook the pickled arm for a pillow. When she woke up in the morning, the woman was mortified to discover she had not only slept with the pickled arm, she had sucked on it through the night. The poor woman was so traumatized that she wouldn't stop sucking on the arm and she was eventually sectioned to a psychiatric institution.

BLOWING IN THE WIND

A woman studying for her PhD in medical theory at Cambridge University had just finished off her thesis. It ran to hundreds of pages and had involved many days of research, so the woman thought it would be a good idea to photocopy everything. She packed the thesis into a box, put the box on the backseat of her car and drove to the college where the photocopier was. However, the woman forgot to close the back window, the box lid was blown off and years of work blew out the window as she drove. It took three weeks for the woman to recover most of the pages, but by then she had missed her deadline and she failed the course.

LIVELY FELLOW

In Salt Lake City, Utah, a dentist was horrified to discover that a patient had died in the chair while he was giving him a filling. Worried about the consequences to his business, the dentist lifted the man over his shoulder, carried him downstairs and left him in the toilet. Ten minutes later, the dentist was stunned to see the man walk into his surgery complaining about a headache. It turned out that the bumping motion of carrying the man down the stairs had been the equivalent of cardiopulmonary resuscitation and the dentist had inadvertently revived the man.

HOOKED UP

In Denver, Colorado, an old man was in hospital for a routine operation. A nurse had given the man a bath and she was drying him, when she found her necklace had somehow become entangled in the man's pubic hair. As the clasp of the necklace was also entangled, she couldn't take the necklace off and no amount of pulling or wriggling would free it. It was at this point that the old man's wife walked in. Before either of them could explain what looked to be a very compromising position, the wife started hitting the nurse and her husband with her handbag. Eventually, other nurses managed to calm the wife down and disentangle the nurse from the old man's genitals. As a consequence, the nurse was told to remove all jewellery while she bathed patients.

NOSE JOB

After years of sleepless nights, a woman finally persuaded her husband to see the doctor about his snoring "which sounded," his wife said, "like an elephant's fart." The doctor gave the man a thorough examination and was surprised to find a rubber stuck up his nose. "My God," exclaimed the man, "a bully shoved that up my nose at school 20 years ago! I must've been so distressed I forgot all about it." The wife was delighted and finally got a good night's sleep, commenting, "He snores just like a pussy cat purring now."

TEAM COLOURS

A hospital in Boston, Massachusetts, had a simple system to cope with organizing the huge number of people working there. It designated people to three teams - the red team, the blue team and the white team (the colours of the American flag) - and everything seemed to run smoothly. However, one day, a black patient innocently asked a passing nurse when a doctor could next have a look at him. Without realizing what she was saying, the nurse replied, "I'm sorry, sir, I don't know, I'm on the white team." Soon after, the hospital changed its system to incorporate colours that could not be misconstrued in any sentence - the azure team, the turquoise team and the magenta team.

SCARED TO DEATH

A group of medical students at Bristol University were talking about a corpse they had seen in the mortuary. Someone in the group dared anyone to sneak into the mortuary and plunge a knife into the corpse. One student said he would do it if the others each bought him a beer afterwards. The student entered the mortuary while the others waited outside. Soon after, the students heard a scream and ran away in terror. The next morning, the student was found dead on the mortuary floor and a knife was discovered sticking out of a corpse. A torn piece of the student's shirt was hanging off the knife. As the student had stabbed the corpse, the knife had caught on his shirt, causing him to think that the corpse was holding him back – he had a heart attack.

NAILING DOWN DISEASE

A man in Texas claimed that God drove a nail through his brain in order to save him for higher things. The man, a joiner in Houston, was messing around with his fellow workers during a lunch break when a nail gun went off, forcing a nail a little over one inch long into his skull just above his right ear. Had the nail penetrated any deeper, it would have damaged his brain and in all probability killed him. The surgeon who removed the nail recommended that the man have a brain scan, just to make sure that no brain damage had occurred. During the course of the scan, doctors discovered a malignant tumour. Surgeons operated to remove the tumour and the man recovered. Speaking about the accident, the victim said: "God put that nail in my brain, but I knew even then that he must have had a reason."

EXTRA BITS

A taxi driver in China was quite rightly proud of his boast that he had never had a reason to visit a doctor in his life. Unfortunately for him, not long after making this claim, he was struck down with severe stomach pains. Unwilling to break his record, he refused to visit his doctor until things became so bad that he was unable to sleep at night and was spending much of the day doubled over in pain. Finally, after constant nagging by family and friends, he went and made first contact with the medical profession. During the initial consultation, the doctor was unable to find anything wrong with the taxi driver and so sent him off to hospital for X-rays. It was then that the cause of his problem was discovered. The cab driver had been blessed at birth with four kidneys – double the usual number – and as a result his intestines had become loaded to breaking point.

MISCELLANEOUS

One of the wonderful thing about a book of urban myths is the fact that all of life can be found within its pages. Every aspect of the human character, every fault, failing and fundamental flaw that we possess as a species can be studied from a distance. For the purposes of this book, we nominated several categories of human behaviour that we felt were worthy of section to themselves, hence the chapters headed Accidents, Animals, Crime, Medical, Motoring, Paranormal and Sex. This chapter, however, deals with those areas of human behaviour that are simply impossible to categorize.

For this reason, the following pages are probably among the more interesting the book. Anyone studying us as a species would gain enough information from the pages that follow to be able to draw quite sensible conclusions about the kind of creatures we really are. I wonder what conclusions would be drawn about the human condition from stories that talk about a curious need to walk around with a salami sausage hanging out of a pair of trousers or the desire to con others into paying for the week's shopping?

A COMIC KILLER

A young boy from Manchester, England, went travelling for a year after finishing his last year of school. After many exciting adventures, he returned home. He was disconcerted to find that his room had been rented out to a university student and all his belongings had been stored in the attic. He asked his mother about his collection of comics, which were his pride and joy and the result of countless years of time-consuming research. His mother turned to him and remarked casually, "Oh, those childish things, I threw them out with all those old stamps and records." When sentencing the boy, the judge stated that although he could understand the boy's anger at his mother's disregard for his possessions, even if they were valued at over £50,000, he could not condone killing her by forcing her to eat her recipe collection.

THE FINAL SLUMBER PARTY

In Miami, Florida, a teenage girl was having a slumber party with a few of her friends. The girls had lots of fun, gossiping, trying on make-up and playing games, before eventually falling asleep. The girl was sleeping on the sofa, but kept being woken up by what she thought was her dog licking her hand. She would shoo the dog away and go back to sleep, but it kept coming back and licking her hand again. Eventually, it stopped and she fell into a deep sleep. In the morning, the girl woke up to find that all her friends and her faithful dog had had their throats slashed, and scrawled in blood on the wall was the message, "People can lick, too!"

THE HEAVY BREATHER

A young woman from Cologne, Germany, was baby-sitting for a wealthy family one Friday night. She had just put the two-year-old son to bed upstairs when the phone rang. The woman answered the phone to hear a man breathing heavily. She slammed down the phone, but the phone rang again. A man on the phone told the young woman what he was going to do to the child, asleep in his bed, and then how he was going to kill her. The young woman, realizing the man must be watching the house if he knew about the child, hung up the phone and immediately rang the police and explained what had happened. The police told her to stay calm and make sure that all the windows and doors were locked and that they would send a police car to the house and also trace the phone calls. After she put the phone down, she secured all the doors and windows, when the phone rang again. The young woman answered and it was the man again, repeating what he said before, but with more elaboration. Suddenly, the policeman interrupted and shouted down the phone, "Get out of there. He's on the extension upstairs." But it was too late.

THE HIDDEN MESSAGE

During the time of the Second World War, a woman from Durham was one of many who had a son in the army. The boy had been stationed in Asia and wrote home regularly as clockwork on a weekly basis. His mother was always overjoyed to receive his letters, so when the letters suddenly stopped coming, she naturally became worried. She soon learned from the Home Office that her son was one of those taken prisoner by the Japanese. A few weeks later, the mother is overjoyed to get a letter from her son. He wrote that he was in a Japanese prisoner of war camp, but that he was being treated well and was in fine health. At the end of the letter, he added, "PS: Steam the stamp off and give it to my little brother for his collection." As the boy was her only son, the mother immediately steamed off the stamp. She was dismayed to see a scrawled message saying, "Help, we're starving!"

POPEYE THE SAILOR MAN

A 13-year-old boy from Warsaw, Poland, was overjoyed when his father brought home a second-hand television set. He would come home from school and watch cartoons for hours. The boy was particularly taken by the cartoon "Popeye" and demanded that his mother cooked spinach for him every night, so that he would be big and strong like Popeye. Of course, the mother was delighted that her son would suddenly want to eat such a healthy diet. This went on for weeks, but the boy was disappointed to find that the spinach had no effect on his stature. Deciding that he obviously wasn't eating enough, he opened all the cans of spinach in the kitchen cupboard and consumed the lot. The boy later died in hospital in a rare case of spinach poisoning.

DOUBLE ENTENDRE

A woman from Bath, England, was just about to take a shower, when she remembered she was supposed to unlock the back door for the decorator, so he could get in to start painting the kitchen. Without thinking, the woman went downstairs without her clothes on. Just as she opened the back door, the gardener came round the back and saw her. Embarrassed and somewhat flustered, the woman told the gardener, "Oh, excuse me, I was just waiting for the decorator." The wrinkled gardener responded with a lascivious wink, "Aye, well, he should have a good time, I'll bet," and started pulling the weeds.

DUD DEALER

An antiques dealer from Penzance, England, went for a walk in the countryside one Sunday. He was taking a shortcut through a farmyard, when he spotted a cabinet in the chicken shed. On closer inspection, he discovered that the cabinet was indeed a Chippendale antique and even though it was covered in chicken droppings, once restored, it could fetch a fortune. The dealer approached the farmer and asked about the cabinet. In order to get a cheap price, the dealer told the farmer that the cabinet legs would be perfect for a table back home. Eventually, the farmer agreed to sell the cabinet for £10 and the dealer told him he would be back the next day with his van to pick up the cabinet. The next day, the dealer drove to the farm and the farmer greeted him. The farmer said, "Oh, yes, I saved you the trouble and removed the legs for you. I even chopped up the rest of it to use as fire wood. Not bad for a tenner, eh?" The dealer duly fainted on the spot.

A REAL TURKEY

In Great Falls, Montana, two kids with nothing better to do decided to play a trick on an old man who tended to fell asleep every evening sitting on a rocking chair on his front porch. The kids found a turkey neck and waited until the old man nodded off. They then crept up and carefully placed the turkey neck in the zipper of the old man's trousers and then hid behind a bush to watch what happened. To their surprise, a neighbourhood cat took an interest in the turkey neck and pounced on the old man. The old man woke up with a start to see the cat nibbling on what he thought was his pecker! The poor old man fainted with shock and the mischievous kids laughed all night.

THE GOOD OLD DAYS

In Atlanta, Georgia, a man in his forties was made to feel truly old one day when he was browsing in a record store. Looking through the rock section for a rare Bob Dylan track, he saw a young boy hold up a copy of The Beatles album Let It Be. He got a shock, when he heard the young boy comment to his friend, "Hey, look, Paul McCartney was in a band before Wings!"

SEDUCTIVE DANCER

A rather big-built young man called Matthew Harris was approached on the street one day by a woman who appeared to be an exotic and rather beautiful belly dancer, complete with a jewel in her navel. This wasn't a regular experience for the man, known to his friends as 'Fatty', and he thought his luck was in – particularly when the woman smiled at him. "Hello," smiled our hero, then realized that the beauty was accompanied by a television crew. "I'm from the local TV news and we're doing a feature. Would you like me to teach you to belly dance on live TV?" In response to which the young man ran away.

HANDY ACCESSORY

Apparently, technical support departments around the world regularly receive calls like this one, placed by a company executive. The high-flier had recently had a new multimedia computer installed on his desk. He had had it for a week, as he explained during the call, and was getting on fine, but he couldn't work out one thing, which was why he was now calling technical support for help. The problem, the executive explained, lay with the cup-holder on the front of his computer. A bit puzzled by this, the advisor asked him to describe this unusual accessory. "Well, it comes out of the front of my computer when I press its button," explained the executive, "but every time I try to put my cup of coffee in it, it goes back in again and won't come out." Patiently, the technical support guy explained the function of a CD-ROM drive to a man in a suit who earned four or five times his salary...

A LITTLE BLUE LIE

An American woman on holiday in New Zealand was staying in a hotel by a lake that is famous for its bright blue colour. She was sitting outside on the terrace of the hotel bar, gazing out over the blue lake, and when the waiter brought her a glass of beer, she asked him how the lake became such a rich blue colour. The waiter, bored of being asked this question throughout the summer, told her that every year at the end of summer the lake is drained and the bottom is painted blue. The tourist seemed to accept this explanation, so the waiter laughed to himself and thought no more of the affair. Towards the end of the summer though, he was surprised to see the same woman at the hotel again. As he took her order he made polite conversation, in which he stated that she must really like the hotel – to which she replied: "Oh yes, and I just had to come back and see the painting of the lake bottom".

EARLY WARNING SYSTEM

In a desert in Nevada, NASA was doing a test run for a future Mars expedition. On the second day of the test, a passing group of local Native Americans stopped to watch the strange goings-on. A NASA official spotted them and went over to talk to them. He explained that the work was in preparation for an expedition to explore Mars. The eldest of the locals considered this and then asked if they could send a message for any life that might be on the planet. Amused by the unusual request, the NASA official agreed, and took a message that the Native American had written in his own language back to the base HQ. Several NASA officials looked at the message, but none of them could translate it. A few years later, an expert on Native American languages came across the message and translated it. It read: "Watch out for these people – they come to take your land!"

LOOK BEFORE YOU FART

A girl was out on a date with the man of her dreams. He was funny, good-looking and rich. He took her to dinner and then to a party and they had a great evening, so she eagerly agreed when he asked her back to his place. Just as they were leaving, she suddenly felt the urge to fart and not wanting to jeopardize her chances, she told her date that she'd meet him at the car. However, she found the toilet occupied and she was becoming desperate. As she couldn't find anywhere discreet to let free the trapped wind, she decided to try her best to hold it in and went to meet her date. Getting into the car, the girl was very relieved when her date said he'd forgotten something at the party and that he'd be back in a minute. When her date was out of sight and out of earshot, she farted loudly and breathed a huge sigh of relief. Not long after, her date returned to the car and he said: "Oh, sorry, have you met John and Catherine? I said I'd give them a lift". Mortified, the girl turned round to see a couple sitting in the back, holding their noses.

CAUGHT OUT

Two students at Oxford University, England were so confident about their psychology final examination the following Monday, that they went into London and partied all weekend with the intention of doing some last-minute revision on the Sunday. However, their night out turned into a drinking marathon and they woke up on Monday morning with stinking hangovers. In no mood to sit an exam, they phoned the Dean of their college and told him that their car had broken down and they wouldn't be able to make it back in time. The Dean agreed to let them take the exam the next day. Relieved, they studied that night and felt confident they would pass the exam. They arrived at the college and the Dean put them in separate rooms, gave each student a surprisingly slim test booklet and told them to begin. The first and only question in the booklet, was "Exactly where did the car break down?" Needless to say, both students failed the exam and had to retake the year.

SHORT CHANGED

A man in England committed suicide by shooting himself in the head, because he found out he hadn't won the National Lottery, when he thought he had. The 28-year-old man believed he had chosen all six of the numbers drawn in that week's lottery, entitling him to a share in the grand prize of £4.8 million. Then he discovered that he hadn't paid for his numbers that week. His dreams shattered, the man took his life. Police investigated the facts, and discovered that the unfortunate man had made two mistakes, rather than one – only four of his regular numbers had been selected in the draw, not all six, so the poor man killed himself because he didn't win £82!

FAX BACK

A company found it was receiving so much junk mail via the fax that its fax machine was continually tied up and no one was able to use it. Realizing that just one marketing company was responsible for these faxes, the manager phoned that company and told the person who answered to remove his company's fax number from their database. However, when a week went by and the faxes had not stopped coming, the manager came up with a bright idea. He printed a page with the word "Virus" written in large letters on it and a second page with a picture of a skull and crossbones. He waited for a space between incoming faxes, placed the first page in the fax and then taped the second page to it to form a continuous loop. He then sent this everlasting fax to the marketing company and left the office for the weekend. The marketing company employees returned on Monday to find its offices knee-deep in faxed messages and acted very quickly to remove the aggrieved company's fax number from its database. Details were transferred to their email list...

TOOTHSOME TALE

Two old men were out fishing off the coast one day in Cornwall, England. They weren't having much luck and were about to turn back when the weather turned nasty. Their boat was getting tossed this way and that, and before long one of the old fellows felt ill and vomited over the side. Unfortunately, the old timer retched so hard that he lost his false teeth along with the contents of his stomach – much to the amusement of his companion. The storm soon passed and the men decided to have another try at fishing. Eventually, one of them hooked a fish and brought it in. He'd caught a large fish, and, before announcing his catch, he decided to play a trick on his friend. He slit open the fish, took out his own false teeth and put them inside the fish. Calling over his companion, he said: "Look at this, I've caught the fish that swallowed your bloody teeth!" The other fellow grabbed the set from the fish and put them in his mouth. After trying to adjust them, he took them out again and said: "Don't fit. They're not mine," as he threw them overboard.

NAMELESS CHEAT

An aged teacher at Eton School was overseeing a history examination one afternoon. When the allotted two hours was up, he told the pupils to put down their pens and went down the aisles collecting their papers. When he came to one pupil, he said: "I won't be collecting your paper as I saw you cheating." He was about to proceed when the pupil stood up and exclaimed haughtily: "Cheating? Do you know who I am?" The teacher, having dealt with many such arrogant pupils in his time, responded disdainfully: "No, young man, I do not, nor does it bear any consequence." The pupil said smiling: "Oh, it does. If you don't know who I am..." and without finishing the sentence, he stuffed his paper into the middle of the pile the teacher was holding and ran out of the classroom.

NO SMALL CHANGE

A young yuppie couple from London bought a dilapidated old church in a small village in Surrey. They spent thousands of pounds renovating it and the wife insisted that they install a light fitting high up in the rafters of the steeple. The husband relented even though he had to hire a qualified steeplejack to do the job, because the steeple was so high. They were pleased with the uniqueness of their new home, particularly the light high in the rafters which had an amazing effect on the surroundings. In fact, the couple became quite proud of the light, and visitors would often comment on it. Six months after it was installed, however, the light bulb blew. The husband realized he would have to hire a steeplejack again. He was furious and shouted at his wife, "Yeah, great idea. It's going to cost £375 every time we have to change the bloody light bulb!"

SWALLOW, NOT SPIT...

A college fraternity house full of males had a raucous party one Friday. The party went on all night and the college girls next door didn't get a wink of sleep. The next morning, they posted an angry letter to their noisy neighbours. That afternoon, the girls received a huge box of doughnuts with a note. The boys were very sorry for keeping them up all night and invited them to come round that evening for a drink. The girls, pacified by the boys' apology, ate the doughnuts happily and then got dressed up for the evening party. When the girls went round, the boys plied them with drinks and begged their forgiveness. One of the girls, returning from the bathroom, decided to have a look at the boys' bedrooms. She was looking around one room when she came across a large photo of the boys, naked with big grins on their faces. On closer inspection, however, she noticed to her horror, that hanging on each boy's penis was a doughnut.

SHORT-CHANGED

A librarian working in Cairo was annoyed when he didn't receive his monthly salary as usual and contacted the office responsible. However, not only was there no record of him on the payroll system, the clerk also told him she couldn't find any record or even barest mention of him anywhere on file. He protested that he had worked at the same library for over ten years, but to no avail. The clerk just replied: "Sorry, we have no record of you or your employment," and hung up. Thinking that this was a temporary error, the librarian borrowed money from a friend and looked forward to being paid two months' wages at the end of the next month. When the next month came and he still had not received any wages, the librarian was furious. He phoned the office again, but the clerk just repeated what she had told him the previous month and hung up. Flabbergasted, the librarian went to the office in person to sort it out once and for all. He shouted at the clerk, "Here I am. I exist. I've been working at the Central Library for over ten years. Here is my contract. I want my money!" Undaunted, the clerk replied: "I'm sorry. We've found your file now." Pointing to a rather short woman at the back, the clerk continued, "Our new assistant couldn't reach her desk, so she took a pile of files to sit on and one of them was yours."

CRASHED OUT

Two British businessmen went to Moscow to finalize a building contract for their company. The men had been forewarned that their Russian counterparts would do anything to jeopardize the deal, so the men were on their guard. Having watched too many James Bond spy films, they set about searching their hotel room for bugs. One man came across a curious-looking bulge in the carpet and on lifting it, discovered a strange box with four large screws attaching it to the floor. Thinking it must be a hi-tech bug, the two men spent a good hour removing the screws. After finally removing the last screw, they were bemused to find that the box was completely empty. The men decided that they were being somewhat overzealous and they went to the hotel bar for a quick drink before retiring for the night. On entering the bar, however, they were greeted by a scene reminiscent of the London Blitz. It turns out that a huge chandelier hanging in the centre of the ceiling had suddenly crashed down, smashing tables and chairs and narrowly missing the shocked patrons. The men put two and two together, made a hasty retreat, went back to their room to pick up their bags and checked out.

BUZZ OFF

This tale is a modern version of David and Goliath… A young man upset the big bully in a small town in redneck Louisiana with the result that the bully threatened that to tear the young man limb from limb that night if he saw him. Knowing from past experience that the bully would do just that, but not wanting to give in to the bully's threats, the eight-stone weakling hatched a plan. Early that evening, he tiptoed by the bully's residence and put a jar of wasps in the back of his car. A little later, as the bully was driving into town, the buzzing angry wasps caused him to crash his car into a tree.

HAPPY TO GO

A top executive of a big American management consultant company entered a lift to find a man openly smoking. The executive told the man that smoking was not permitted anywhere in the building and instructed him to extinguish his cigarette immediately. Instead of doing anything, the smoker just shrugged, mentioned that there were no ashtrays and continued smoking. Furious, the executive grabbed the man's cigarette, threw it on the lift floor and stamped it out with his shoe, only to see the man casually light another one and continue smoking. Incensed, the executive asked the man what his monthly salary was. The man replied: "About £700." The executive counted out £700 and handed it to the man: "There's a month's salary. Consider yourself sacked – dismissed with immediate effect." The man stepped out of the lift, smiled and said: "Hey, thanks. Actually, I don't work for you, I just came in to use the bathroom."

THE GOSSIP

A young man at an exclusive university college decided to settle a score with a fellow student by writing a scurrilous attack on the person's character and submitting it to the widely-read student magazine. The young man had forgotten the first rule of gossip columns, which states that those who tell tales are usually the ones who are shot down in flames. When the next issue of the publication appeared, he was horrified to find an article accusing him of being 'a mincing pseud and universal hate-figure' of the college.

SICK MISTAKE

A financial adviser who worked in the centre of London returned to his house in the suburbs after a few hours of drinking with his colleagues, travelling on a train that was so full of people that he had to stand in the middle of the carriage. At one point, the effect of drinking on an empty stomach and the lurching motion of the train began to make the man feel sick. Realizing that he suddenly had to vomit, but knowing he wouldn't make it to the window in time, he opened his briefcase and discretely puked there. The next morning, the woke up with a serious hangover, but suddenly remembered the events of the night before. Rushing down to stop his wife putting his sandwiches in his briefcase he found that the briefcase was devoid of vomit. Clearly, he had used a fellow traveller's briefcase on the train – a traveller who must have had a most unpleasant surprise...

KNUCKLE DOWN

A couple celebrated their anniversary at a restaurant that had not long been open. They both ordered dishes with exotic French names, selecting a good bottle of wine to go with the meal. As the wife was enjoying her main course she suddenly choked and coughed up a small bone. To avoid embarrassment, she discretely wrapped the bone in her napkin and shoved it in her pocket. After the meal, the couple went on to a bar for a drink. The woman, feeling a sneeze coming on, took the napkin from her pocket, only for the bone to fall out and drop at the barman's feet. The barman, who was studying medicine, examined the bone and declared to the red-faced wife: "That's interesting. This appears to be a human knuckle bone."

ENGAGING STORY

A young man, wanting to propose to his girlfriend, needed a romantic setting for the purpose. Looking in the local newspaper, he came across an advertisement for a restaurant which seemed ideal. The advert read: romantic restaurant with panoramic views of countryside and an atmosphere that will create an explosive reaction for lovers. The man collected his girlfriend the next evening and they drove out to the exclusive restaurant. On parking the car and approaching the restaurant, the young man was devastated to find a mass of disgruntled people leaving. On entering, he saw the reason why: the panoramic view included a nuclear power station, and all over the walls were models of weapons of mass destruction. Realizing that this particular restaurant was perhaps not the ideal place to propose marriage, he took his girlfriend home, got a Chinese takeaway, and later that night proposed in the less explosive atmosphere of his bedroom.

COCK UP

Times were bad and the manager of a sweet factory that supplied rock candy to shops all over England had been advised to lay off staff. First to go, so far as the manager was concerned, would be a young lad who was always rude and usually had a lazy approach to his work. The manager was surprised when, instead of cursing him as expected, the lad worked his day's notice and departed with a warm farewell. A few days later, everything became clear when he received an angry phone call from a big customer in Brighton. The customer was fuming that a consignment of rock, which was supposed to read "Brighton Rock" instead read "Brighton Cock!"

GOT HER NUMBER

A British diplomat lost his job when the government changed after an election and told his wife that they would have to be careful with money for a while. The wife was saddened to see her husband in such a state and decided to sell some of her possessions to ease their financial plight. One item she decided to sell was very precious to her and she only wore to very special occasions. It was a bronze pendant that had been presented to her during a visit to Bangkok. There was an inscription on the pendant written in Thai, but everyone she asked said they couldn't translate it and changed the subject or make excuses to leave. So the diplomat's wife was more than a little ashamed when she came across the item at the auction with the description, "19th Century bronze medallion with inscription in Thai, translates to 'Legalized Prostitute Number 283, Bangkok.'"

TELLING PORKIES

An American couple planned to go to Colombia for a two-week holiday and sought the advice of a friend who was always showing off his language skills and bragging about all the countries he had been to. He gave them tips on where they should go and on here to stay, and also taught them a few key phrases in Spanish. The couple took a room in a hotel and then went out for some food. After finally selecting a restaurant, the man decided to try out the Spanish phrases their friend had taught them. When he asked the waiter for the menu, the waiter just stared at him before running off and coming back with the manager. The man repeated the phrase to the manager. Again, the response was startled stares, before they ran off and came back with the chef. The chef asked the man in English: "Why do you think the manager owns a pig – and why in God's name, if he did, do you think he would want to have sex with it?"

CHRISTIAN VALUES

Students studying for a Theology degree arrived at their final exam to find a note on the door saying that the examination would take place in a room on the other side of the campus. The students all rushed to the other room to find a bedraggled fellow blocking the doorway and begging for money. All the students except one barged by the fellow and took their seats. The one student chatted to the beggar and then gave him £1, before taking his seat. After the exam was over, the students discussed the questions they had been asked and all seemed quite satisfied that they must have passed, but when they received the results, they were shocked to discover that all but one of them had failed. Confronting their professor, the students were told that they failed because they had ignored the beggar at the door and in so doing confirmed their disregard for Christian virtue. The one student who had demonstrated Christian charity became a very popular priest. The others apparently became politicians, lawyers and advertising executives.

SMOKE BUG

In Surrey, a middle-aged couple who had seen the last of their children leave the nest rarely went up to the top floor of their house where their children had had their rooms. One day, the mother noticed an odd chirping noise coming from the top floor and, scared it was some horrible creepy crawly, she went and got her husband. The husband, not the most courageous of men, crept slowly up the stairs and searched all the rooms for the source of the noise, but he couldn't work out where it was coming from. The next day, the husband called in an exterminator. The exterminator arrived and after some fruitless searching, suddenly worked out what the noise must be. He went downstairs and informed the couple that the batteries in their smoke alarm needed changing.

BONELESS IDIOT

A newly wed English couple were looking forward to spending their first Christmas together. On the day, to the bemusement of her husband, the wife took the turkey and cut the bones out of the bird's legs before placing it in the oven. The husband asked her why she mutilated the bird and she explained that she was merely doing what her mother always did when preparing to roast a turkey. The couple had invited their parents for the Christmas meal and when they were all sat round the table, the wife took the opportunity to ask her mother why she cut the bones out of the turkey drumsticks. The mother replied: "Oh, that's because the oven at home was so small, it was the only way I could get the big bird in."

...FROM THE VILLAGE, NO DOUBT

In Beverly Hills, California, a woman had spent the morning working in the garden. Feeling hot, bothered and a little dirty she went to have a shower. Five minutes into the shower, she heard the doorbell go. She was about to put on her dressing gown when she heard the doorbell ring again and a man shout out: "Blind man!" Assuming it was a blind man begging for money and not wanting to soak her bathrobe, she ran downstairs and opened the door. The man at the door just stared at the naked woman, before spluttering out: "Uh, hi. Erm, I'm here to put the blinds in."

ADOPTED MOTHER

A young man from Cambridge, England, went into a supermarket to buy a pint of milk and six eggs. As he looked for the milk, he noticed a middle-aged woman staring at him with sad, forlorn eyes. He turned away, grabbed a pint of milk and went in search of the eggs. When he found the eggs, he turned around only to see the same woman staring at him. Somewhat disturbed, he hurried towards the cashier, but remembered that he had run out of toilet paper and so returned to the main part of the store to find some. Arriving back at the cashier, he saw that the woman is in front of him in the queue with a cart that was full almost to the brim. The old lady finally said to the young man: "I'm sorry for staring. You see, you look just like my son who died only a few weeks ago." She sniffled and added: "Yes, the same hair and eyes. Just like him." As she packed her groceries, she whispered to the young man: "Could you do a grief-stricken mother a favour? Could you just say 'Goodbye, Mum' as I leave?" The man agreed and when she left the store, struggling with four heavy bags of shopping, he shouted out "Goodbye, Mum." His feeling of worthiness was short-lived however, when the cashier told him the bill was £94. "There must be a mistake," he exclaimed pointing to his three items, but the cashier replied: "Your mother said you'd take care of her shopping, too."

REWARDING DUMP

A woman went shopping in the centre of Bethesda, Maryland, one weekend, and in the middle of her trip had an urgent need to go to the toilet. Each shop she tried didn't have a public toilet and eventually, she was so desperate, she entered a funeral home to use their facilities. Having used the toilet, the woman went to leave the building, but on the way, she passed a darkened room with a coffin containing a man's body in the centre with flower arrangements on either side. Feeling a little guilty about using the toilets, the woman entered the dark room and signed the guest book. There was no-one around and the woman breathed a sigh of relief as she left the funeral home. A few weeks later, the woman received a letter from the dead man's lawyer informing her that the deceased had left $100,000 to be divided between the people attending his funeral. As she was the only person to show up, she got the lot.

EXPENSIVE MISTAKE

A woman travelling on an underground train in London spotted an expensive cashmere scarf on the floor of the carriage just as a man was leaving. Quick as she could, she grabbed the scarf, threw it out of the door onto the platform and shouted after the man as the train doors closed. Feeling good about herself, the woman resumed her seat in the carriage, but soon realized that people were staring at her. Then one of them, an old man said to her: "Madame, are you insane? That was my scarf you just threw out the door."

TOWERING LIE

An American man was on holiday in Paris and decided to hire a personal tour guide to help him look around the city. The tour guide first took his client to the cathedral in Montmartre where the tourist asked him how long the cathedral took to build, to which the reply was: "about ten years". The American retorted: "Gee, in America, we would have had this up in ten months!" The next attractions were the Arc De Triomphe, Notre-Dame and the Louvre, and at each place the American asked the same question and then retorted with a boast of how quickly the monument would have been built in America. When they arrived at the Eiffel Tower, the American asked the guide: "Wow, what is that?" and the exasperated man replied flatly: "I have no idea – it certainly wasn't there yesterday".

SPECIAL OFFER

An up-and-coming fashion designer from Melbourne, Australia, was eating a meal in a Chinese restaurant when she noticed the Chinese characters in the menu and decided they would make a good design on a dress. She copied out a few lines in her notebook. A few weeks later, she had finished her first design incorporating Chinese characters. The woman decided to wear the dress to a party at the community centre that weekend. As it happened, a few Chinese people from the area were also at the party and several started sniggering and nudging one another when they saw the designer dress. Not one to be the subject of a joke, the woman asked what they found so funny. He explained that the characters on her dress read: "This dish cheap but very tasty."

NOT SO SWEET

A young man, who grew up in the back-of-beyond in Louisiana, decided to move to New Orleans and start a new life. He moved into a house with a couple of guys and managed to get a job as a waiter in a restaurant. On the man's first day at work, the manager noticed that his new employee was making tea by ripping open a teabag and pouring the contents into a cup before adding hot water. The manager showed the young man how to dip the teabag into the cup of hot water to make a proper cup of tea. A week later, the manager was pleased to see the young man make a cup of tea for himself as he had shown him. However, he nearly died laughing when he noticed an unopened sachet of sugar floating on the surface.

HONEY, I'M HOME

A group of young men from Manchester, England went on a day trip to the holiday resort of Blackpool. They spent most of the day seeing all the sights and trying out the roller-coaster rides, and then found a bar in which to get a few drinks before returning home. In the bar, they befriended a man who looked like he'd had a few too many drinks when they met him. The near-drunk was glad of an audience and told the group of daytrippers joke after joke before finally passing out. Unsure what to do, one of the group searched the man's pockets and eventually found his home address in his wallet. Seeing that the man was also from Manchester, the young men decided to do him a favour and take him home with them. Back in Manchester, one of the group volunteered to take the man home and on reaching the address knocked on the door. The woman who answered was startled to see the man and said: " 'Ere, mate, what the bloody hell is he doing 'ere? He's supposed to be on his honeymoon in Blackpool this weekend!"

LONG JOURNEY

A man from the south of England had too many drinks in a bar on the way home from work one day and lost track of the time. Fortunately he just managed to catch what he thought was the last train of the day out of London to his home town of Basingstoke. However, he soon found out that while the train he had boarded passed through Basingstoke, it didn't stop at Basingstoke. He had climbed on an express train that went straight on to Southampton. He decided that if the train slowed down enough at Basingstoke, he would probably be able to jump off. The train did slow down at the station, and the unlucky traveller grabbed his bag, jumped on to the platform and then began running alongside the train to reduce his speed. As the next coach passed him, he was suddenly yanked back onto the train by another man who said: "Lucky I saw you running. Didn't you know this train never stops here?"

WEDDED BLISS

A bride and groom from Perth, Australia, were most surprised when the priest marrying them began to insult them and act very strangely indeed. The priest called the groom "a stupid oaf with the intelligence of a baboon" before comparing the bride to a kangaroo's arse. In front of the stunned congregation, the priest then broke into a rendition of Madonna's 'Like a Virgin' before turning round, lifting up his cassock and mooning at the stunned couple. The priest then smiled at the couple and said: "I'm a priest-o-gram courtesy of your best man. Good luck. May you have lots of furry, little children," and then ran off to be replaced by the somewhat embarrassed genuine priest.

WHOLE WORLD'S CHOKING...

In England, the National No Smoking Day can provide people with an excuse to act in outrageous ways – for instance, dousing anyone caught smoking with a bucket of cold water. In Argentina, things have been known to become even more extreme. A masked man calling himself The Big Smoke chose No Smoking Day to terrorize smokers in Buenos Aires by forcing anyone he caught smoking, at gunpoint, to eat the whole pack of cigarettes. As each victim chewed and gagged on a mouthful of tobacco The Big Smoke took the opportunity to preach about the harm smoking can do and the dangers of passive smoking. Although some victims said they would give up smoking, most appeared to be desperate for a smoke after their ordeal. Rumours that The Big Smoke was employed by the government have been consistently denied by officials.

GREEN AS THEY GET

A sound engineer announced that he had discovered that the sound quality on compact discs improves significantly if the thin outer edge of the CD is coated with a green marker pen. Music lovers were heartened by the news until they found out that the sound engineer was a green fanatic. The engineer had painted his whole house various shades of green, owned a green Volkswagen Beetle and had previously declared that green M&Ms were known to have aphrodisiac qualities.

HI MOM! HI DAD!

A young man had just begun his first year at Leicester University in England and was sharing a house with several other students. One day, the student was in a hurry to get ready to go out, so he left a couple of the friends with whom he shared the house chatting in his room and went to have a shower. After his shower, he still heard voices in his room, so he decided to surprise his friends by whipping off his towel, kicking open the door and, while holding his pecker in his hand, leaping dramatically into the room shouting: "Bang, bang, you're dead!" Unfortunately, the voices did not belong to his fellow students, but to his girlfriend and her parents who had made a surprise visit.

DOUBLE OR QUITS

A taxi driver was given a pair of tickets to go see a West End musical in London, but he realized that the show had been given appalling reviews and was reluctant to waste his time by going. Hating to see anything go to waste, the taxi driver left the tickets on the back seat of his cab, hoping that someone would take them and make use of them. However, at the end of the shift not only were there no takers, but someone had placed another pair of tickets on top of them.

IT'S ALIVE!

A poor old lady from Tirana, Albania, was not looking forward to the winter months, so was delighted when she found a cheap, down bedcover in her local market. She took it home and spread it over her bed. When she looked into her bedroom later, she was mystified to see that the bedcover had fallen off the bed, but she just shrugged and threw it back over the bed. That night, the old lady got into bed and looked forward to a warm night under her new bedcover. However, in the middle of the night, she woke up shivering and saw that, again, the bedcover had fallen to the floor. Curious, the old lady got out a pair of scissors and carefully cut open the quilt. She was disgusted to discover that the feathers used to fill the bedcover had not been washed and were stained with blood. On closer inspection, the old lady was horrified to see hundreds of maggots all over the feathers. Obviously, the wriggling maggots had kept causing the bedcover to fall of the bed. The poor old lady burnt the bedcover and had a cold, harsh, sleepless winter.

MYSTERY VOICE

A council housing officer from London was transferred to another district and spent his first week in his new job getting acquainted with the housing estates that were now under his jurisdiction. His usual approach to visiting a block of apartments was to go to the top floor and work his way down, and when he made his last visit of the day he followed his usual pattern. Entering the lift he pressed the button to take him to the top floor, but nothing happened. Deciding that the lift must be broken, he was about to leave when a young girl entered and shouted "Fourth floor!" The lift went up to the fourth floor. The housing officer was amazed that the estate should have a voice-activated lift, but when he shouted "Sixth floor!" the lift went up to the sixth floor. Back at the office, he asked his colleagues when the council had installed hi-tech, voice-activated lifts on estates. His colleagues all looked at him as if he was crazy but one of them knew what he was talking about and laughingly explained. The lift controls were broken and a man was paid by residents of the apartment block to stay on top of the lift. When people shouted what floor they wanted, he connected the two appropriate wires and the lift went to that floor.

MISTAKEN IDENTITY

A well-known public school in England came under investigation after the headmaster allegedly assaulted a school inspector. Several boys had been caught smoking and had been sent to the headmaster's office for punishment. While they were waiting outside, a school inspector paid an unannounced visit and waited for the headmaster at the end of the queue of boys. The headmaster eventually emerged from his office, admonished each pupil in turn for smoking, and gave each of them a whack with his cane. When the headmaster came to school inspector he can't have been concentrating for, despite the man's moustache, he assumed that he was just an unusually tall pupil. Before the man could protest, he thrashed him three times on the hand with the cane.

ZIPPEDY DOO DAH

In Toulouse, France, a girl invited her boyfriend home for dinner to meet her parents. The boy really liked the girl, so he was very eager for the meeting to go well, so he expressed interest in the parents' respective jobs and tried to show that he cared for their daughter very much. The evening seemed to be going fine by the time they all sat down for dinner. The mother served dinner and told him that she had cooked pheasant, which at that time of year was very hard to get hold of and very expensive. The boy was about to start eating, when he looked down and realized his zip was undone. As inconspicuously as he could he fastened up his zip and, remembering what his mother told him about washing his hands, he asked if he could use the bathroom before eating. Unfortunately, the tablecloth had got caught in the zipper, so as he rose from the table and walked away, he took the cloth with him, complete with all the plates full of food, the glasses, bottles and condiments. To the boy's horror, everything smashed on the floor. There was an awkward silence, before the boy fled in tears.

DUNKING DUMP

An interesting lawsuit was brought against a German tourist by a Greek hotel owner. The hotel owner sued for damages, alleging that the man's actions had caused several other hotel guests to leave. In his defence, the German stated that his actions were a direct result of eating the food served in the hotel. As it came out in court, the tourist had been lounging in the hotel swimming pool when he suffered a bout of stomach cramps. Unable to get out of the pool in time, he lost control of his bodily functions while he was still in the water. Before he knew it, a young girl had spotted the brown slick circling him and alerted the other guests. It didn't take long for the pool to empty. Eventually, the red-faced man escaped into the toilets and cleaned himself up. He emerged only to face the wrath of the hotel owner: the incident had caused several guests to check out. The man blamed the sudden bowel movement on the mussels he'd had for lunch in the hotel restaurant.

SOMETHING BLUE...

A stag night prank went terribly wrong in Switzerland when the best man slept through his alarm. Sadly, the groom-to-be had made the lethal mistake of passing out the previous night and his friends decided it would be really funny if they stripped him and left him handcuffed to the pulpit of the church he was to be married in. The plan was that the best man would get to the church early enough to rescue the groom, but not before he had woken up and spent a few worried hours. That was not to be... instead, the guests arrived at the appointed time to find the groom waking up in a daze and completely naked. Covering his nudity with the priest's prayer book, the groom escaped to the vestry and put on a cassock. Thankfully, the bride had a sense of humour, and declared: "At least, he got here on time". Although the groom was dressed in an unorthodox manner, the marriage went ahead almost on time.

GOOD NEIGHBOUR

A woman had lived in an apartment in Manhattan for most of her adult life, but her landlord was determined to get rid of her in order to put up the rent. One day, the woman noticed a new tenant moving in next door to her and she invited him round for a drink. However, the man told her he belonged to a religious sect which forbade him to be alone with a woman and closed the door on her. The woman gave the matter no more thought until strange things began to happen. Every night at about 2:00am, she heard what sounded like someone being tortured and the man chanting. Occasionally she would spot the man carrying a heavy, black bag upstairs. One morning, she noticed that the bag was leaking what looked like blood and, somewhat scared, she called the police. The police told her there was nothing they could do and the woman began thinking about moving out. One day, however, a letter to her neighbour was delivered to her by mistake. Hoping for evidence, the woman steamed open the envelope. She was shocked to find a cheque for $200 for the man's "portrayal of a religious freak" and immediately realized that the landlord had hired an actor in an attempt to drive her out of her apartment. The woman confronted her landlord and threatened to report him if he didn't reduce her rent, which he duly did.

THANKS FOR THE TIP

A butcher from Lyons, France, used to delight in shocking people by sticking a salami in his trousers and exposing it. When his victim commented on the exposed protrusion, the butcher would take out a cleaver and lop off the tip. The joke went a too far one day, when, spotting a female friend he hadn't seen for years, he popped an extra large salami down his trousers. Leaving the tip sticking out, the butcher approached his friend who commented: "My God, you must be pleased to see me, you're huge!" Whereupon, the butcher replied: "Ah, I have no control over it." He took out his cleaver and lopped off the tip. His friend promptly had a heart attack and her husband successfully sued the butcher for several hundred thousand francs.

JUST THE TICKET

In Oxford, England, a man who had been buying several lottery tickets every week for the last two years was in his local bar as usual, watching the lottery numbers being drawn on television. On this occasion, it turned out the man had got five of the six winning numbers and stood a good chance of winning tens of thousands of pounds, so he bought everybody in the room a celebratory round of drinks and had several himself. Dreaming about how he would spend his fortune, the man passed his ticket around for people to inspect. However, when he eventually came back to him, it wasn't the same ticket. Someone had switched it on him!

COOKED-UP STORY

A young boy wanted to impress his mother by baking her a cake on her birthday. The boy's mother returned home from work early that evening to find him hovering outside the door to the kitchen, so she asked her son what he was doing. He explained that he was just following the recipe for cake. Slightly bemused, she asked the boy what the recipe told him to do. He explained that the recipe said to fold the dough into a cake tin, which he had done, and then instructed "Leave room to rise" so he had left the room. He told his mother, who was straining to stop herself laughing: "I left it over two hours ago and nothing's happened!"

SHAKESPEAREAN COMEDY

The Royal Exchange Theatre in Manchester, England, staged a production of William Shakespeare's play Richard III. In the final act, the actor playing Richard III exclaims in a booming voice the famous line: "A horse, a horse! My kingdom for a horse!" One evening, a man in the audience decided to comment: "'Ere, mate, I've got a horse". There were a few titters in the audience, when the actor replied: "I asked for a horse, not an ass!" This quick adlib brought the house down and the production was an overwhelming success.

OUT ON A LIMB

A Japanese couple on holiday in New York went to eat in a well-known restaurant in lower Manhattan. They had both finished the meal when the woman told her husband that she would go to the bathroom before they left. The man paid their bill and waited for his wife to return. However, after 30 minutes, he became concerned and asked a waitress to check on his wife. The waitress returned to say the toilets were empty. The man looked in the toilets himself and then looked all over the restaurant, but there was no sign of his wife. The police were called in, but after weeks of investigation, there was no clue as to what had happened to the man's wife and he was forced to abandon the search and return to Japan. Two years later, a friend of the man phoned him. He had just returned from a trip to Bangkok and he had seen his wife performing at a freak show there. The husband couldn't believe his ears and asked his friend how his wife could possibly be in such a show. His friend sadly explained that her arms and legs had been amputated.

FRESH MEAT

Residents of remote Chinese villages on the border with North Korea seemed oddly reluctant to bury their dead. When asked to explain why this was so, many villagers replied that evil spirits came in the night and removed the bodies of their loved ones and took them away to Hell. One journalist investigating this story decided that this explanation seemed less than plausible – not least because the bodies were removed from above rather than below – and set out to investigate what was happening. Having arranged for an empty coffin to be buried with much show and ceremony, he took up a hidden position and waited to see what happened. He did not have to wait long, as a small group of North Koreans crossed over the border from their country, which was in the grip of famine, and dug up what they thought was a fresh body. Apparently, the food situation had become so desperate that they had resorted to cannibalism in order to feed their families.

TIMELY REMINDER

A man from Eccles, a town in the north of England, decided that when he died he wanted to be cremated. There was nothing unusual in that, but he made an addition to his will at the last moment. Having carefully set aside a certain sum of money, he requested that his ashes be placed not in an urn, but in a rather elaborate egg timer, which was to be kept in his wife's kitchen after he was gone. With the help of a very skilful glassblower, his wife was able to carry out her husband's last wish and he now sits on her kitchen table, helping her to boil eggs whenever he is required.

TOIL AND TROUBLE

A group of witches in Romania have banded together and formed a union in an effort to drive out the charlatans who they feel are bringing the good name of witchcraft into disrepute. They claim that the bogus witches, all of whom say they are descended from the great witch Omida – who died 30 years ago – are unable to perform the tasks required of a working witch and so have set a special challenge. From now on, anyone who wishes to be recognized as an authorized witch must be able to prove their abilities to lift evil spells, have the strength to cast out devils and be capable of predicting the future correctly.

POOPY LOVE

When two very young Polish lovers were refused permission to marry by their respective parents, they decided to do what any other couple in their position would do (if you believe Shakespeare) and checked into a cheap hotel with the intention of committing suicide. Before doing so, they had stopped off at their local chemist, who knew both their families well, and asked for the strongest poison he had in his shop. The chemist suspected that they might be up to no good and so instead brewed up the most powerful laxative he could create. This was particularly unfortunate as the room they had rented at the hotel did not come with an en-suite bathroom and they had thrown the key to the locked door out of the sixth floor window after locking it from the inside. After making their final farewells to each other, the couple proceeded to swallow the entire contents of the bottle before settling down on the bed to die. Three days later, and after numerous screams for help, the couple were finally discovered by a maid who had come to clean the room. Unfortunately for the maid, the room needed rather more cleaning than she had imagined. The manager of the hotel stated later: "The room stinks. The walls are caked and even the ceiling is splattered. You cannot even see through the windows". The couple abandoned their plans to marry.

COLD, WET NOSE?

Many years ago some friends decided to have the party to end all parties. Five were sharing a house at the time and they decided that they would move most of the furniture out, take up all the carpets, contact every DJ they knew and turn the whole event into a night to remember. By midnight the house was shaking. The hallway became so packed that the only way to get up or down the stairs was to go outside, climb on to the kitchen roof and go in through the bathroom window. By 3am there were bodies everywhere and people were starting to burn out. By 5am there were just a few brave souls left, and everyone was looking for somewhere to sleep. Or rather everyone except one lonely girl in a corner. Nobody knew who she was (the students certainly hadn't invited her) but she seemed determined to kill herself. She sat there rather forlornly taking pill after pill from a bottle she had found in the bathroom. Everybody felt sorry for her, not least because no one had the heart to tell her that she was trying to commit suicide by taking the dog's worming tablets.

UNFEASIBLY LARGE UNDERWEAR

A commuter in the Japanese city of Tokyo caused mayhem on the subway when he accidentally triggered his newly-patented invention. His invention was a pair of self-inflating rubber underpants that would serve as a life-saver in times of flood or when lost at sea. Unfortunately they were designed to grow to over 30 times their uninflated size, and did so when the man set them off while rummaging around inside a pocket in an attempt to find a mint. This occurred during the rush hour and commuters on the already overcrowded train were crushed against the doors when it soon became clear that there was nowhere to hide from the expanding underwear. When asked why he was wearing the pneumatic knickers on a train, the man replied that his greatest fear in life was to be caught in a severe flood in case it caused him to be late for work. A fellow passenger saved the day in the end by puncturing the pants with a pencil.

CUPID STUNT

A gang of boys were doing their best to show off in front of a group of girls they had spotted on a street corner. Being boys, they decided that the best possible way to impress the girls was to ride their bicycles in a dangerous and reckless fashion (jump forward ten years and most of them will still be trying to do the same thing in their Ford Escorts). All went well to begin with and the girls were even humouring the boys by pretending to be impressed but then one junior stuntman decided to go just that little bit too far. Having got up a fair bit of speed, he climbed on to the handlebars of his bicycle and tried to ride along standing upright. For a creature who had barely learned to walk upright, this was a little over ambitious. Inevitably, the bike folded under him and he suddenly found himself with half a handle bar up his butt. Now this really did impress the girls, who fell about with laughter until the ambulance took him off to hospital.

TERRORIZING TELEPHONES

Any story that starts with two friends and a rifle can only have a limited number of endings, but the end of this one may well come as a surprise to some of you. The two friends took to the streets one night armed only with a severe lack of intellect and a loaded .22 calibre rifle – a lethal combination. Our boys decided to go hunting…for telephone boxes. Between them they made a number of holes in half the town's call boxes before one of them decided to try a trick shot by firing over his shoulder at one of the vicious phone boxes. To his surprise he managed to hit the target. Not to be outdone, his friend decided to go one better. Standing with his back to the target, he bent over, pointed the gun between his legs and waved goodbye to the phone box. Unfortunately the bullet ricocheted off the box and right back at him, making him one of the few men in history to have shot himself in the butt with his own rifle.

LOVE PACT

The Swedes are a curious people. They seem to combine a talent for beauty and a love of peace with a morbid fascination with death. One could be forgiven for believing that suicide is almost a way of life in Sweden. A classic example of a Swedish-style suicide concerns the sad case of a man and his girlfriend who had made a pact to die together after they discovered that ABBA were not planning to re-form in the near future (or some similar tragedy). Having found a pleasant location in which to die, near a popular tourist spot, the man, by agreement, strangled his girlfriend and then set about strangling himself. He discovered to his horror that this was not going to kill him and so he went looking for other means to end it all. Unfortunately, he soon realized that he had lost the courage to take his own life and instead handed himself over to the police. They had little choice but to charge him with murder, for which he eventually received an eight-year prison sentence – he appealed against it on the grounds that it was too lenient.

CHEAP TRAVEL

Two families – we'll call them the Smarts and the Dumbs – met on a train journey to Manchester, England. Members of the two families started to talk to one another and it soon became apparent that the Smarts had bought only one ticket between them for the journey. Shortly before the ticket inspector came round, the Smarts headed off to the toilet. After collecting the Dumbs' tickets, the inspector banged on the door of the toilet and shouted: "Tickets, please". A single hand emerged – complete with ticket – and the inspector, having satisfied himself that all was well with the world, clipped the proffered ticket and carried on down the train. The Dumbs were deeply impressed by this feat of cunning and in the course of the rest of the journey they arranged to meet the Smarts for the trip home. Sure enough, on the journey home the two families met again, only this time the Dumbs had bought just the one ticket - the Smarts hadn't even bought one. Just as the Smarts were beginning to explain how they were going to get around the problem, the ticket inspector was spotted heading their way. The Dumbs rushed into the toilet and a short while later there was a knock at the door. "Tickets, please" said Mr Smart before pocketing the Dumbs' ticket and joining his family in another toilet.

TEST CASE

A psychology class that had been learning about the effects of positive reinforcement on test subjects (people who are told they are doing well and so consequently do well) decided to try an experiment on their teacher. One half of the class smiled appreciatively at everything he said and managed to look interested throughout the entire class. Meanwhile, the other half of the class pretended to ignore the lesson and looked bored. Within a few minutes, the teacher began to focus all of his attention on the enthusiastic group while ignoring the other half of the class. Later that day the students wrote up their observations and were rewarded with top marks.

PHILOSOPHICAL POINTS

This urban myth, which is concerned with the activities of university philosophy departments, has transcended the status of mere myth and is now quite rightly considered to be an urban legend. Philosophy courses are famous for asking difficult questions like, 'If you took a boat apart and built it again of the same material, would it still be the same boat?', but at least that allows room for argument. Imagine the poor students in the hellish philosophy exam where the one and only question was "Why?", to which the only correct answer was "Because".

DRINK IT ALL UP, NOW

A young boy went to stay at his grandparents' house one weekend. Waking in the middle of the night with a terrible thirst, he went downstairs to the kitchen. Half-asleep still, his eyes lit on what he took to be a bottle of homemade lemonade, a particular treat for him, as his grandmother used regularly to make a mean lemonade. It was only when he opened the bottle and took a deep swig that he realized his error. The bottle was actually his grandfather's phlegm jar, in which the old man would relieve a particularly nasty lung infection. Still, as the boy picked a long, stringy piece of crouton-like phlegm from his mouth, at least we may be certain that the midnight thirst was not the main thing bothering him any more.

BARREL OF LAUGHS

When a building worker was applying for compensation after an accident he was asked to write down what, in his opinion, had been the cause of the accident. On the form he wrote "lack of forward planning". His insurers were puzzled by this and contacted him for clarification. It seems that the man had been given the task of lowering a huge amount of bricks to street level after too many had been taken up to the top of a building to complete a job. Having set up a pulley, he tied a rope around a barrel full of bricks, wound it through the pulley and dropped the rest of the rope the ground. His plan was to lower the barrel via the pulley, an operation he would control from the ground. Unfortunately, as the barrel began to descend it soon became clear that, even with the assistance of the pulley, he was getting lifted off the ground. Like a true hero he held on for dear life, smashing his kneecaps as he passed the barrel on his by now rapid journey up the side of the building. When the barrel hit the ground it smashed open and the bricks fell out with the result that he began to head groundwards at a remarkable speed. He hit the pavement with a thump, breaking both ankles but finally letting go of the rope, which caused the remains of the barrel to come crashing down around his ears.

UNUSUAL ARTEFACTS

The staff at a museum of natural history were amused when a young boy sent them some of the objects he had found in his parents' back garden. They felt compelled, however, to write to the boy to explain to him that he had not, in fact, discovered anything that would be of real interest to them. Of the tiny human skull he had discovered they wrote that, to the best of their knowledge, prehistoric man did not play with Barbie dolls and that ancient relics of this sort are usually made of bone, not plastic. They were, however, particularly impressed with the bone he had found which had, he claimed, once belonged to a junior Tyrannosaurus Rex. Unfortunately, after close investigation and a quick polish, they were sorry to report that he had in fact discovered the remains of an adjustable spanner. They finished by thanking him for his efforts and urging him to carry on his important work.

MOTORING

One of our greatest failings as a species is that, for the most part, we stopped evolving around 5,000 years ago. This may seem like an odd claim to make, but the fact is that while all the other creatures on this planet have evolved to cope with the challenges the modern world has presented to them, we have merely changed the modern world to suit ourselves. This did not cause us too many problems until the invention of the automobile.

While there might have been road rage problems back in the days of the horse and cart, the consequences of such behaviour were diminished by the fact that few people travelled any faster than about 11 miles an hour – about the same average speed as London traffic today. Unfortunately we now have a situation where high-speed, half-ton horseless carriages are being driven by creatures who, in evolutionary terms, belong in caves. We are simply not equipped to deal with motor vehicles and as a consequence some of the strangest and most unacceptable behaviour that human beings have ever indulged in occurs while in command of these vehicles.

A TASTE FOR VANILLA

A woman from Rochester, Michigan, took her car to the garage and told the mechanic that it was behaving strangely. She explained that every time she went to the local grocery shop to buy vanilla ice cream, the car would fail to start on her return. She continued that if she bought any other flavour, the car started fine. The mechanic thought the woman must be mad, but he agreed to try to repair the car. However, on examining the engine, he could find nothing wrong, so he decided to go buy some ice cream himself to test the woman's story. The mechanic drove the car to the grocery shop and bought a large tub of vanilla ice cream. Like the woman had told him, the car refused to start. Eventually, the mechanic worked out that the grocery shop took longer to get vanilla ice cream than any other flavour because it was the only one that wasn't pre-packed. It seemed the car didn't start because it remained idle for the amount of time it took to buy vanilla ice cream.

A TESTING EXPERIENCE

A boy from Marseilles, France, was taking his motorbike driving test. He had been doing very well so far and he was confident he would pass. The examiner wanted to test his emergency stop and he told the boy to drive around certain roads and when the examiner jumped out in front of him, he was stop immediately. The boy sped off on his motorbike and drove around the streets the examiner had told him to, but after 15 minutes the examiner had still not appeared and the boy was getting concerned. He drove around and around for another 15 minutes before finally giving up and returning to the testing centre. At the centre, the boy found out what had happened. It seemed the examiner had heard the sound of an approaching motorbike and stepped out, only for it to be the wrong motorbike and for it to hit him head on. The poor examiner was treated in hospital for several injuries, whilst the boy was allowed to pass his test.

EMERGENCY PICNIC

In the mountains between France and Spain, there are some hairpin bends on major mountain roads which are notorious accident blackspots, especially for truck drivers. So on most of these bends, uphill safety ramps have been placed for trucks with failed brakes to make an emergency stop. One day, a truck driver with a particularly heavy load was driving from Paris to Madrid along the mountain road. He had managed the ascent fine, but as the truck sped downhill, the driver realized he had lost his brakes. As the truck careered down the busy road, the driver flashed his lights and tooted his horn, swerving all over the road to avoid the other cars. The driver was relieved when he eventually saw a sign stating that there was a safety ramp just around the corner and he successfully manoeuvred the speeding truck around the tight corner. As he went up the ramp, however, he ran right into a family of American tourists having a picnic, killing them all instantly.

CRUISING CAMPERVAN

A Japanese couple travelling around New Zealand decided to hire a camper-van to get the most of their trip. They drove out of Auckland and ended up on a long stretch of road. An hour or so into the journey, the wife told her husband she was going to lie down for a while. The husband continued driving, but shortly after, he realized he desperately needed to go to the toilet. The husband, not wanting to stop, noticed that there was a "Cruise" option on the gears and assumed that it must be the equivalent of an auto-pilot. He quickly put the van into the cruise mode and ran back to the toilet. Naturally, before he had even taken down his trousers, the campervan careered off the road and straight into a river before hitting a rock and coming to a sudden halt.

SNAP HAPPY

Here's one to make you think twice when trying to elude the law… A man from Chicago, taking his prized Porsche out for a spin, was caught speeding by a roadside camera. The resulting penalty notice arrived in the post. It included a photograph of the car and the date and speed of the offence and demanded payment of a fine within seven days. The motorist chuckled to himself and decided to play a little practical joke on the police. He duly sent a photograph of a cheque to the unsuspecting police. A few days later, he received a letter from the police. Inside was a big glossy photograph of a prison cell. Sure enough, the speeding motorist got the hint and paid the fine.

SOCKET TO ME

This is for all the drivers out there who think it's cool to hang their arm out of the car window whilst cruising around. A man was doing just that while driving in his convertible along a Californian highway one sunny day. With his shades on, the stereo blasting and his arm hanging languidly out of the window, the young man failed to notice a shovel protruding from a flat-bedded truck coming the other way. As they passed, the shovel struck his arm and ripped it out of the socket. With barely a swerve, the man continued driving seemingly unphased. He drove for over ten miles until he stopped at a petrol station, shocking other customers as they spotted his bleeding shoulder. It wasn't until he attempted to unscrew the petrol cap on his car that he looked down and realized his arm was missing. He told doctors at the hospital that he had no memory of the accident.

JUST THE ONE LIFE...

One night, a truck driver was driving through the outskirts of Chicago to deliver his last load of the week. Suddenly, a cat ran out into the road in front of him. The driver slammed his foot on the brakes, but he was sure that he was too late. He got out of the truck and looked underneath, but it was too dark to see anything. Retrieving a torch from inside the cab, he spotted the cat writhing on the sidewalk. Close to tears, the man did the decent thing and ended the cat's agony with a swift blow with a hammer. Then he climbed back into his truck and was about to depart when an old lady opened his cab door and began screaming at him. Thinking she must be the owner of the poor cat, he tried to explain but she was hysterical and started hitting him. Eventually, the woman calmed down, and told him that she saw him run over her neighbour's cat, stop the truck and then hit her own cat with a hammer.

SWAP TILL YOU DROP

A young couple moved into a quiet suburban enclave. Their neighbours, another couple, invited them round for dinner along with several other couples who lived nearby. As the night wore on and drinks were consumed, the new couple learnt that all the guests indulged in wife-swapping – and they were asked if they wanted to join in. Although hesitant at first, they agreed. Each husband threw his car keys into a hat and a wife would blindly pick out a key and go off with the owner. The young husband threw the key to his Mercedes into the hat with the others and the choosing began. Each wife took turns and eventually, his wife was paired off. Her husband was upset to see how excited he wife was but didn't say anything, instead hoping that he would be pleased with his partner. However, one of the wives said she felt ill and left, leaving him the odd one out and without a partner. The young man sulked all the way home and was infuriated to see that his Mercedes had gone. Wife-less and car-less, the man crashed out. The next morning, he was pleased to see that his car had been returned, but distressed to find in it a note from his wife telling him that she was leaving him.

LOAD OF BULL

A young woman from Manchester, England, had an experience learning to drive that would put anyone off ever driving again. Her father thought he would take her out for a spin in the country and let her drive along the quiet country lanes. Around Macclesfield, he stopped the car, let his daughter take the wheel and, after a few false starts, she was driving smoothly. As she started to gain confidence, she even put her foot down but slowed again and shifted down to second gear as she approached a bend. Unfortunately, she turned the corner to see a bull standing right in the middle of the road. She slammed her foot on the brakes, but it was too late and she ran right into the poor animal. On discovering that the bull was dead, the young woman burst into tears. It didn't help when a distressed farmer pulled up and asked them if they had seen, Big Red, his champion Hereford bull.

OLD FART

A 17-year-old boy from London was taking his driving test and felt confident that he would pass. Everything was going smoothly until it came to doing a three-point turn in the road. As he was about to reverse, the examiner farted loudly, causing the youngster to stall the car. The examiner made a mark on his pad and told the boy to drive on. A little annoyed, the boy continued, only to have the same thing happen when he was attempting to reverse park. The furious boy got out of the car and stormed off in disgust. The examiner was about to tell him that it didn't matter and that he had passed the test anyway, when a lorry driving past smashed the open car door off its hinges. Needless to say, the examiner reversed his decision and failed the sensitive teenager.

SMART PARKER

A young man had just passed his driving test and was returning home to tell his friends and family the good news. On his way, he decided to stop at an liquor store to buy a celebratory bottle of champagne. He couldn't find a parking place anywhere, so he parked halfway on to the pavement, rushed into the store, bought a bottle of champagne and rushed out again. On returning to his car, however, he was concerned to see a policeman standing by the vehicle. Sheepishly, the boy approached the policeman and told him he'd only just parked it there. The policeman replied, gritting his teeth: "I know. You parked on my bloody foot!"

THE LORD'S WAY

A God-fearing Irish woman was driving her family home from their weekly jaunt to the church fund-raising fair, when she overheard her 14-year-old daughter tell her 12-year-old brother that God wasn't real. The woman looked at her daughter through the rear-view mirror and said firmly: "Of course, God is real. God is everywhere." To which the daughter retorted: "Then why don't we see or feel him?" The mother frowned and said: "Well, let's see, shall we?" She took her hands off the wheel and said aloud: "God, drive us home!" With no apparent divine intervention, the car spun out of control across the road and rolled over the embankment. Visiting his family in hospital afterwards, the husband said to his wife: "Well, it's a miracle that none of you were killed."

COPYCAT SPIN

A group of Italian tourists had just been on the infamous Shotover Jet in Queenstown, New Zealand, and were driving back to their hotel. The driver was going over every detail of the apparently nail-biting experience. He went on about how close the jet-boat driver got to the canyon walls and how fast he was going. However, when he went on to describe how the jet-boat driver put his hand in the air to signal that he was going to spin the boat around, the Italian couldn't help but try out the manoeuvre himself in the car. To the surprise of his companions, the driver put his hand in the air and slammed on the handbrake. Unfortunately, the driver had somehow forgotten that he was not in the middle of a quiet river but on a very busy road. Luckily, there were no fatalities in the resultant 15-car pile up.

SCENIC ROUTE

An old man from Bristol, England popped out to visit his daughter who lived about ten minutes away by car. The old man's memory was a bit erratic and, as a result of some road works, he got a bit confused and ended up on the M5 motorway going north. Eventually, ten hours later, the old man arrived at his daughter's house via Birmingham, where he'd driven round and round Spaghetti Junction, and then up to Manchester, before turning back. His distressed daughter quipped: "Next time, I'll visit him."

SLOW AND STEADY

A middle-aged woman was thought to be one of the safest drivers in California, but this was due more to being very careful than to her expertise. On one occasion, the woman had just been to town to do some shopping and was emerging from the car park, when she came to a busy junction. The cars kept coming in both directions and every time she went to turn left, another flurry of traffic would prevent her. Six hours later, the traffic began to slow, but the woman had fallen asleep and by the time she woke up, it was the morning rush hour. After about an hour of morning traffic, the woman plucked up her courage and went for it, only to crash straight into the side of a police car.

WE ARE SAILING...

A senile old couple from Wellington went to visit the newly-opened National Museum, Te Papa. As the museum was very popular the couple found it difficult to find a parking place, but eventually they discovered a new multi-storey car park about 15 minutes away. They spent a few enjoyable hours exploring the museum, but when they left, they couldn't find the car park. They went up and down the streets, but the car park had vanished. Thinking that they may have fallen victim to some massive car-stealing scheme, the couple went to the police. When the couple showed the policeman where they thought they had left the car, he immediately knew what had happened. Trying to keep a straight face, he told them that what they had taken to be a multi-storey car park was in fact the Wellington to Picton ferry. Three hours later, the ferry returned and the couple picked up their car and drove home.

ROOF PARTY

A young man from Newcastle got completely drunk at a friend's party and ended up passing out in what he thought was the bedroom. A few hours later, he woke up to see buildings and lamp posts flying past on either side at an alarming rate. At first he thought he was still drunk and his head was just spinning, but when he looked down, he realized he was on the roof of his friend's car. It seems in his seriously inebriated state, he had mistaken the garage for a bedroom and the car for a bed. The driver became aware of the extra passenger's existence when his hitch hiker was sick all over his windscreen.

PREMATURE CELEBRATIONS

A young man who had just passed his driving test celebrated with his family over a bottle of champagne. He then went to the pub to join his friends for a few more celebratory drinks, foolishly taking his car. After one too many, the boy staggered to his car and went to reverse out of his parking place. Suddenly, there was a crunch. The boy had reversed straight into the side of a passing car. Bleary-eyed, the boy was more than surprised to discover that the driver of the passing car was none other than the driving test examiner who had passed him earlier that day. The young man was subsequently banned from driving for 12 months.

MAKING THE BOSS CROSS

A policeman from a small town in Arizona pulled over a motorist for speeding. The man tried to explain why he was in a hurry, but the cop was not in a good mood and arrested him for obstruction. Still protesting, the man was taken to the police station and thrown into the jail. The bad-tempered cop then growled at him: "The Chief will sort you out, ya moaning minnie. He's at his daughter's wedding but he should be back soon." "I wouldn't bet on it, you moron," said the man through gritted teeth, "Seeing that I'm the bridegroom."

ANYTHING YOU SAY

A policeman was directing traffic on the M1 motorway in England after a serious car accident. At one point, an old lady in a beaten-up Fiat Uno slowed down and asked the policeman: "Is there anything I can do to help? I was a nurse in the war, you know." The policeman thanked her but said: "The best thing you can do, madam, is drive off around those cones ahead." He was astonished, moments later, to see the old lady drive off and ever so slowly zig-zag around each cone until she disappeared over the horizon.

DRIVE, HE SAID

A man studying at Southampton University in England decided to save money by hitch-hiking home for Christmas. The student wasn't having much luck, possibly because of his unwashed, unshaven and unkempt appearance, but eventually a car stopped at a junction and he leapt in. The old woman driving asked where he was going, but she wouldn't be drawn into conversation after that, so the student passed the time counting the number of cars that overtook them. On reaching London, the student was surprised when the old lady asked him directions to his house. Pleased to be saving yet more money by not having to take the tube, the student directed her to his house. On reaching his house, he thanked the woman for the lift, whereupon she replied: "Lift? I thought you had taken me hostage!"

HIGH ROLLER

A man had nothing but mechanical trouble and breakdown after breakdown in the two years that he owned his car. Fed up, he decided to try and sell it. He gave it a good clean and polish, tuned up the engine as best as he could and put an advertisement in the local paper, describing the car as a good runner with one careful owner. The man realized that the 500,000 miles on the clock might not look so good and decided to fix it at a more appealing level. On opening up the speedometer, the man was surprised and somewhat peeved to find a note wedged into the back that read: "Oh, no, not again. Shouldn't I be consigned to the scrap heap by now?"

SHOWN THE WAY HOME

An old fellow was driving home after a day in the English countryside when a blanket of fog suddenly descended. The fog was so thick, that the man could hardly see 20 feet ahead. He was about to pull over and wait until it lifted, when he spotted a car ahead and, thinking the driver must know where he was going, latched on to the car's tail lights. After driving several miles, the car in front turned left and then proceeded to make a series of turns before suddenly stopping. The old man saw his opportunity, got out of his car and asked the other driver where he was. The driver coldly replied: "Well, this is my driveway. Now, bugger off!" Leaving the old man standing there in shock, he vanished into his house.

NEARLY ESCAPED

A man was driving along a stretch of motorway late at night and decided it was time he pushed his new Porsche 911 to the limits. Putting his foot down and hurtling down the deserted motorway at 150 mph, the man suddenly lost control and the car crashed into the central barriers and turned over. The driver miraculously escaped unharmed and, rather shakily, went to cross the road to phone the emergency services. Unfortunately, as he crossed over, a speeding Skoda came around the corner and hit him.

OLD BANGER

Two factory workers from Moscow were out for a weekend hunting trip in the wilds of the tundra. As they were returning to their cabin that evening, their old car suddenly stopped and all the lights failed. Eventually, the driver worked out that a fuse had blown and, with the aid of a torch, tried to find a temporary replacement. After half an hour of fruitless searching, his companion shouted out: "It is OK, comrade. I will fix it." He placed something in the fuse holder and the car spluttered into action. About a mile down the road, there was a sudden loud explosion and the car died again. The driver, somewhat pale, asked his companion, "What did you put in there?", to which his friend answered: "I just used a bullet from the gun, why?" Painfully, the driver explained: "Well, comrade, I have just been shot," and pointed to his groin.

ONE BUMP TOO MANY

A woman from North London drove to a party in South London with the intent of getting a taxi home if she got too drunk. A few drinks later, however, and ignoring her friend's wise advice, the woman decided she was in a fit state to drive home. After struggling to drive out of a tight parking spot and ignoring the fact that she'd bumped the car behind, the woman drove away and eventually, with a few hazy close shaves, she made it home. She struggled into the house and immediately blacked out on her sofa. She was woken in the early hours of the next morning by someone persistently ringing her door bell. On opening her front door, she was startled to see an annoyed policeman, who proceeded to question her about her activities on the previous night. He told her that she would be prosecuted for drunken driving and hit and run damage to another car. Curious, the shaken woman asked the policeman how he could be so sure it was her. The policeman smiled and held up the woman's licence plate: "This was found embedded in the other car, madam."

EASY MISTAKE TO MAKE

An old woman was driving home to Eastbourne on the south coast of England one day when she noticed what looked like a microwave oven abandoned on the side of the road. The woman stopped to pick it up hoping that her son, who was an electrician, could make it work. The woman was so excited with her find that she tried to get home as fast as she could and didn't notice that she was speeding. Inevitably she was pulled over by the police. The police officer noticed, on the backseat of her car, the object that the woman had picked up. It was not a microwave, but a speed-monitoring camera. Despite the old woman's protests, the police arrested her and charged her with theft of government property.

THE BLOW-OUT

Driving home from work one evening, a man from Johannesburg had a blow-out on the motorway and pulled over to change the tyres. The man had just started jacking up the front of his car, when another car pulled over and a young man got out and offered to help him. The man was happy to get any help he could and readily accepted the young man's offer. However, he was surprised when, instead of grabbing the spare tyre on the ground, the young man took a jack out of his car and began jacking up the rear of the car. So he asked the young man to explain what he was up to. "Well, I thought you could have the front wheels and I could have the rear wheels," came the reply. The driver had innocently pulled over on a road notorious for car thefts and car-stripping.

PUSHING HARD

An Palmerston North, New Zealand, a man had a very old car that was always breaking down and constantly needed to be push-started. However, the man loved the car and refused to trade it in for a new one. One day, he was in town and, as usual, the car stalled. He waved down a passing motorist and asked the driver, a teenager, if he would be prepared to push-start the old car with the front end of his. The teenager said that he would be happy to.

The man warned the teenager that, as the old car had an automatic transmission, he would need to get up to at least 35 mph or it wouldn't work. Unfortunately, the teenager took the man literally and before the man knew it, the teenager had reversed his car half a block away and accelerated to 35 mph as he drove towards him. His clapped out motor was a write-off and the man had to walk home.

A MERRY NOTE

In Rome, Italy, a young woman had just returned to her car after doing some last-minute Christmas shopping. She got into the car but, as she reversed out of her parking place she knocked into the car behind, causing a big dent in the front bumper. The driver of the other car was not around, but several people had witnessed the incident, so the woman wrote a note and left it under the windscreen wiper. When the driver of the other car returned, he noticed the dented bumper and found the note. "Sorry about the dent. I would leave my name and address, but my insurance premium is high enough as it is. Merry Christmas."

SLEEPING BEAUTY

A couple on a caravan holiday in France had spent a few days in La Rochelle before going to their final destination near Bordeaux. Wanting to arrive in Bordeaux before dark, the husband left early in the morning and decided to let his wife continue sleeping in the caravan. After an hour of driving, the husband pulled into a small garage to refuel. Unknown to him, his wife took the opportunity to freshen up in the garage bathroom. Meanwhile the husband paid the bill and, still thinking that his wife was asleep in the caravan, drove on to Bordeaux where he realized his error. The abandoned wife, meanwhile, dressed only in a skimpy negligee and with no money, was fortunate enough to come across a helpful young man who had a motorbike. The biker put her on the pillion seat and roared after the husband. The husband was astounded to see the biker pull up alongside him, together with his half-dressed wife.

ROAD HOG

In Ireland, a man was driving along a country road. Up ahead, he saw an attractive woman drive round the corner towards him. As the woman passed, he smiled at her, but the woman just shouted at him: "Pig!" The man quickly retorted: "Witch!" and sped off. However, when he turned the corner, there, standing in the middle of his lane, staring right at him, was a large pig. The man managed to swerve out of the way, but ended up in a ditch.

BETWEEN THE EYES

Three friends from Kansas City were riding their motorbikes one night on an open highway. One of them decided to really go for it and accelerated away from the other two. Eventually, he turned around and as he saw their headlights in the distance, he decided to give his friends a scare by riding in-between them. He sped up and went to drive through them, but didn't realize, until it was too late, that the headlights belonged to a truck that had overtaken his friends. He died instantly.

DRIVING AT A PINCH

In Los Angeles a driving instructor was so exasperated with a student, who had failed his driving test 12 times, that he concluded that extreme measures were called for. In subsequent driving lessons, whenever the student made a mistake, the instructor pinched him hard on the leg. The instructor was so surprised by the student's improved performance, that he entered him for another test within two weeks. Unfortunately the student failed again. When the instructor asked the student what had gone wrong the student replied: "Well, I was doing the reverse parking and I was waiting and waiting for the examiner to pinch me, but he didn't, so I crashed into the car behind."

AUTOMATIC TRANSMISSION

A boy from Oakland, California, was given a brand-new, automatic transmission car for his eighteenth birthday. Eager to show off the car to his friends, he thanked his parents and drove off. He found his friends in a deserted parking lot and one of them challenged him to a race. Seeing it as an opportunity to test his new car, the boy agreed. The two boys lined their cars up, revved their motors and waited for another boy to signal start. As the flag dropped the challenger pulled away fast and, try as he could, the boy could not keep up with him. Desperate to win, the boy spotted R on the choice of gears and, in a moment of stupidity, thought it stood for race. The accelerating car suddenly spun out of control, and crashed into a post. For anyone else who doesn't already know, the R on an automatic stands for reverse.

MISTAKEN IDENTITY

A Californian biker entered a roadside cafe, carrying his helmet and gloves. He ordered some food and drink, and sat down in the non-smoking area. Just after his food arrived, a man at the next table lit up a cigarette. The biker politely pointed out that they were sat in a non-smoking area and asked the man to either move or put out the cigarette. The smoker angrily grunted, but stood up and left. However, as he walked past the biker, he noticed his helmet and, concluding that the Harley in the forecourt must be his, he pushed it over. Unfortunately for the man, the Harley actually belonged to the café's cook, a large, hairy, leather-clad guy, who saw what was done to his prize possession and went after the man with a meat cleaver. Meanwhile, the biker finished his meal, grabbed his helmet and gloves, walked round the side of the building to his Honda 550, and rode away.

FIRST APPEARANCES...

In Holland, a group of leather-clad, rough-looking bikers pulled into a petrol station and entered the shop. The shop assistant was worried that the bikers would cause trouble so, when a group of smartly-dressed kids showed up, he was noticeably relieved. The bikers grabbed what they wanted, paid for it and left without a word. The shop assistant turned to the group of kids and said: "Thank goodness, you showed up. There's no telling what they would've done!" At which point, one of the kids pulled out a shotgun and ordered the shop assistant to hand over all the money in the till. The shop assistant vowed never to give in to stereotyping again.

FLAT OUT

A father and son had gone to a baseball game at Candlestick Park in San Francisco. The father had driven there in his BMW but, on leaving the game, they couldn't find the car where they'd parked it and, after searching everywhere, they concluded that it had been stolen. The father reported the theft to the police and caught a taxi home with his son. Just as they arrived home, there was a big earthquake that affected the whole Bay Area. The next day, the father received a phone call from the police. His car had been found flattened by a landslide caused by the earthquake. The car thief was also found in the car, crushed to death.

SQUASHED LIKE A BEETLE

An accident was reported late one night on the autobahn from Berlin to Munich. Two lorries had crashed head on at high speed, killing both drivers. The cabs of both lorries had fused together with the force of the impact and the wrecks were towed away as one piece to a junk yard. A week later, however, a horrible stench was emanating from the wreck and the junk yard attendant was told to separate the two cabs. The cabs were prized apart and there, flattened between them, was a very thin Volkswagen Beetle with four very dead occupants.

FATAL ACCIDENT

A woman had got used to her husband staying out late and getting drunk, so she wasn't too surprised when she heard the screech of brakes outside late one night. The next morning, she found her husband snoring away on the sofa downstairs. She roused him and told him he only had 20 minutes to get to work. The man got up quickly, washed his face and ran out of the door. His wife, suddenly realizing that her husband would have to pick their children up from school, ran out after him. She took one look at her husband's car and fainted. Embedded in the grill of it was the dead body of a seven-year-old girl.

LOVE IN CHAINS

A man from Milan, Italy, was extremely proud of his classic Ferrari sports car. It had taken him years to restore it to mint condition and he was very precious about it, only taking it out on special occasions. Wary of its attraction to thieves, the man kept it locked up in his garage and used heavy chains around its frame which were secured with impenetrable locks to pins in the wall. Every night, he left the car facing into the garage, all locked up and covered with a tarpaulin. One especially beautiful morning, the man decided to take his prize out for a spin and went into the garage. He removed the tarpaulin and discovered the car all locked up but facing in the other direction. On the windshield was a note: "We can have this car any time we want it." It was signed "…a good car thief."

MAD MOONER

A bored driver who was travelling alone decided, for reasons known only to himself, to make the journey a little more interesting. To this end, and while still driving along, he dropped his pants, stuck his butt out of the window and began to "moon" at the drivers who were travelling in the opposite direction. All went well until he decided to get a bit more ambitious – or rather get a bit more of his backside out of the widow. Having jammed the accelerator pedal down with his car jack, he hung right out of the window and would probably have carried on baring his behind for the rest of the afternoon had he not lost his grip and fallen backwards on to the road. He landed relatively unhurt (apart from some very unusual skid marks) but was forced to watch as his car carried on some way down the road, with his trousers attached, until it came to rest...in the back of a police car.

WASHDAY BLUES

A 35-year-old woman died recently while attempting to wash her car. She went out to her garage to wash the vehicle but decided that it would be best to move the car on to her driveway where it would be easier to get at. Having first put the car into neutral, she pushed from the front and eventually it began to roll backwards. Soon, however, it became obvious that the vehicle was no longer under her control. As quickly as she could, she rushed to the rear of the car and attempted to stop it with her own body weight. Unfortunately the car had now gathered momentum and, despite her best efforts, continued to roll backwards. In her desperation to stop the vehicle, she ignored her own safety and was run over for her troubles. Having flattened its owner, the car then carried on across the road before running up a neighbour's driveway and colliding with the front of his house.

COLD COMFORT

A police officer in the States decided to stop a speeding driver late one winter's night. Pulling in behind the driver, he climbed out of his patrol car to have a word with the offender, leaving the engine of the patrol car running because the night air was so cold. He had a word with the driver, took his licence and walked back to the police car to run a check on the documents, but was unable to get back into his vehicle. Deciding to pretend at least to be a nice guy, he walked back to the motorist, delivered a short sermon and sent him on his way with a warning never to speed again. Looking around, he noticed that there was nobody about. His radio was in the car and there was not a pay phone in sight. Before too long, however, another police car turned up to find out why he wasn't answering his radio. Just as he was about to talk to his colleague, an urgent call came through and the brother officer had to speed off. "Get in the trunk to keep warm," he said to the freezing policeman, "I'll come back and pick you up later." Realizing that this was the only way he was going to survive the cold, he did so, only to find himself locked in until his colleague returned, five hours later, with a large audience in tow.

PARANORMAL

There are not so many paranormal Urban Myths, but those that do exist are some of the funniest and occasionally the most disturbing tales around.
The main problem with tales of the paranormal is that they fall into just two categories: the ghost story and the "no sane person would ever believe this" story. There is actually an abundance of ghost stories, but almost all of them finish with the words "and when I looked round the traveller/old lady/hitch hiker/ghostly figure was gone".
For this reason a couple of stories have been included that might reasonably have been put in the crime section of the book. These are tales of grave robbing and cannibalism that, although at first appearing to have paranormal causes, ultimately turned out to be the result of far more mundane criminal activities. That said, the paranormal itself is beginning to acquire an air of the ordinary.
Things have moved on a long way from the days of ghoulies and ghosties and long-leggety beasties who went bump in the night.

GHOST OF A CHANCE

A man was driving home along the A34 to Oxford, England when he spotted a pretty woman thumbing for a lift. Not one to refuse such an attractive offer, the man stopped the car. The woman got and he asked her where was she going, but she didn't say a word – she just pointed ahead. As the man drove, he tried to make conversation, but the woman remained silent. As they were approaching a junction on the outskirts of Oxford, the woman signalled to the man to stop. He stopped the car and the woman opened the door, smiled at him and mouthed "Thank you" before getting out. The man watched her walk up the road and then enter a house. He was about to drive off when he noticed that she had forgotten her coat, and had left it on the back seat. Thinking the woman might have done this on purpose, so that he would pay her a visit, he parked the car by the house he'd seen her enter. He rang the doorbell and was surprised when an old lady answered the door. He told her that the young woman who lives in the house forgot her coat in his car. The old lady glared at him and said slowly: "You must be mistaken. There is no young woman here. My daughter was killed in a car accident on the A34 two years ago."

WALKING DEAD

Apparently, this was a common occurrence, but still understandably heart-stopping. Family and friends had gathered for the funeral of a young boy killed in a gangland slaying in Little Rock, Arkansas. The priest was just about to start on the last rites, when a young boy came upon the scene. Suddenly, women were screaming, men were gaping in shock and the mother fainted. Confounded, the priest asked a nearby mourner if this outburst was a ritual within the community. The mourner said in a wavering voice: "No, Father. That boy who has just walked in, he's the one we're supposed to be burying today." A pragmatist, the priest managed to calm people down and after much discussion realized what had happened. He worked out that the boy's mother suffered from glaucoma and when she was called to the police station to identify the body, she mistook the dead body for her son.

STAKED OUT

A group of tourists on a sight-seeing trip around Edinburgh, Scotland, were taking in the splendour of the city and, at the same time, being educated about Edinburgh's darker past – the focus of the tour was a ghost walk, a trek around haunted sites. They paused to contemplate the site of a particularly gruesome murder and to be told about the ghostly events that had occurred there since the slaying. While this was going on, a woman dressed in a cape appeared carrying a wooden stake, which she proceeded to plunge into the chest of the tour guide. The tour guide crashed to the ground and the tourists, assuming that this was a spectacularly well-acted piece of street theatre, applauded wildly. Unfortunately, the scene they had witnessed was not a piece of theatre but an actual murder carried out by a deranged woman who had been driven insane by the constant noise of tour guides droning on outside her window.

LIKE A VIRGIN

A church in a small town in Ireland, gained notoriety when the statue of the Virgin Mary was reported to speak to visitors. Rumours began when a local woman praying to the statue said she heard the Virgin Mary tell her that Jesus would return to the people very soon. In no time at all, flocks of people were turning up at the church and every now and then, the statue would talk about the return of Jesus and what the people should do to prepare for it. At one point, hundreds of people were gathered in the church. They all waited with bated breath to hear the Virgin Mary speak. Eventually, the statue began to speak: "Jesus will...". Suddenly there was an ear-splitting whine and the statue continued: "Shit, I spilt my cup o' tea!" The priest turned scarlet red and the people began murmuring. It didn't take long for people to figure out that a local businessman had planted a radio transmitter in the statue and his wife had made the pronouncements in a bid to boost tourism to the town. Funny that most people didn't question the Virgin Mary having an Irish accent.

POLTERGUIDE

A group of New Zealanders touring Scotland arrived in Stirling, a place that held them in awe with its rich history and heritage. They parked their car and wandered around, when they came across an old Scottish man, complete with his clan tartan and bagpipes. He spoke to them in a strong brogue accent, claiming that he was from the Mackenzie clan that was defeated by the Cameron clan in the area. The group was delighted to have met such an interesting man and chatted for some time before saying their farewells and driving on. Later in the day they stopped at some souvenir shops and stumbled across the old Scottish man again. They gave him a knowing nod, bought a few trinkets and, waving goodbye to the Scotsman, continued their journey. They stopped a mile or so up the road to admire a plaque dedicated to the "War of the Two Clans" and there he was yet again. Bewildered at how he had got there before them, they asked him to join them for a group photo. Back in New Zealand, the group had the photos of their trip developed. But on looking through them, they were shocked to see that the group photo that was taken of them with the old Scotsman showed them standing by the plaque with their arms round an empty space.

PARANOID

A man from South Dakota was obsessed that the world was going to end in any number of ways. As far as he was concerned it was just a matter of what got us all first from a long list that ran from alien invasion to the impact of a giant meteorite. One day he was listening to radio signals from outer space when he saw a shower of asteroids land in his backyard. The asteroids were bright green and the man, worried that they were radioactive, retreated to his specially-built bunker and radioed for help. Eventually, the police turned up to investigate, only to discover that the luminous, radioactive asteroids were in fact green balloons from a nearby fair.

ALIEN ABDUCTION

In a small town in Texas, a mother was worried when her not-too-bright son failed to return from work. She told the police, who organized a search party that combed the surrounding area, but they couldn't find any trace of him. Two days later the young man turned up looking the worse for wear and talking about being abducted by aliens. He told interested reporters that he had been walking back home from work when he had met the aliens, who had taken him back to a brightly-coloured room with strange, loud music playing. He went on to describe how the aliens had forced him to eat food which burnt the back of his throat and to drink a foul-tasting liquid before he blacked out. He remembers nothing after that until he woke up in a field with a splitting headache and made his way home. One sceptical reporter, investigating the details that the man had given him, discovered a little bar full of Mexicans near the field where the man had woken up and he realized what had happened. The Mexicans had taken the man in and plied him with hot spicy food and tequila. The man had got drunk and passed out and, on relating the story, he used the US immigration term of "alien" to apply to the Mexicans.

TV ADDICT

A 12-year-old boy watched the film Poltergeist at a friend's house and was unduly influenced by its content. One night, his mother found him sitting in front of the television after transmissions had finished for the day staring at the "snow". However, any attempt to remove him from the television and put him to bed, ended up with the boy in hysterics. This went on for a few nights and the parents had no idea what to do. They asked their friends and one of them suggested they put a radio transmitter in the television set and try talking to him through that. The parents did just that and, putting on a ghostly voice, the father talked to the boy. They were delighted when the boy responded. When the father told his son to go to bed, they were even more delighted when he obeyed. It became a nightly ritual and the parents found life became a lot easier for them, because anything they asked of their son, he would do. He got up for school without complaint, helped make meals, did all his homework and all his chores, as long as they told him to do things through the television.

SEX

There are those who would claim that the word "myth" is simply a polite way of saying "lie". It is certainly the case that the word myth, when applied to historical events, takes on a respectability that the words "made up" certainly do not possess. But it is in the field of sex, even more so than in history or politics, that myths are most likely to be found.

It begins with teenage boys and their tales of daring on first dates - what passed at the time for little more than a quick fumble around becomes a sexual encounter of near legendary proportions by the time it has done the rounds of the school playground. And so it goes on into adult life.

There is barely a man alive who can resist the temptation to view himself as some sort of sexual athlete, when in fact most men are little more than the equivalent of Sunday-league footballers in the bedroom. Women, on the other hand, tend to be a little less forthcoming about their sexual encounters, preferring instead to exaggerate the more romantic elements. Unless, of course, they are in the exclusive company of other women, in which case they can be relied upon to be far more candid than most men would ever dream of being. Read on, but bear in mind that most of these stories owe more than a little to the wholly human art of exaggeration.

LIKE FATHER, LIKE DAUGHTER...

A young woman had been single for so long that she decided to try out a virtual sex chatline on her computer. Calling herself Sexy Sue she discovered that it was more than enjoyable. After a few weeks trying out various chatlines, she found someone called Hunky Hank and got thoroughly turned on by his virtual intercourse. Their chats became more and more regular and in time they were turning each other on every night. After nearly a year of frantic cybersex, they both agreed that they were finally ready to meet and so they arranged a suitable rendezvous at a hotel. A little nervous but very excited, Sexy Sue arrived at the hotel earlier than arranged so that she could prepare a romantic atmosphere in their room. She placed candles all around the bed and scattered rose petals around the room before undressing and lying on the bed in anticipation of Hunky Hank's imminent arrival. Soon after there was a knock on the door. Sexy Sue asked: "Is that you, Hank?" and receiving the sought-after affirmative answer, panted: "Come in, come in!" Hunky Hank walked in to see Sexy Sue sprawled naked on the bed, but when their eyes met, it wasn't lust but horror on their minds – Sexy Sue was Hunky Hank's daughter!

NO SPITTING, NO EATING, NO...

The 6:04pm London to Brighton train is almost always packed, as it was one hot summer day – commuters and travellers were squashed next to each other on the seats and in the aisles of carriages. A young couple in one corner seemed to be more packed still… about 15 minutes into the journey it became apparent that they were actually having sex. Men with bowler hats and umbrellas pretended not to notice, young women giggled, old men and women tut-tutted quietly, and others averted their eyes, but noone said a word or tried to put a stop to this display of exhibitionism. A few minutes and some stifled gasps later, the couple reached their crescendo, tidied up their clothes and relaxed. It was only when both the young man and young lady lit up post-coital cigarettes that they sparked a reaction. One polite gentleman leaned towards them and said: "Excuse me, but this is a non-smoking carriage."

LOOK BEFORE YOU SUCK

A helpful husband started to fix a leak under the kitchen sink one weekend as his wife left to go out shopping. On her return she saw two legs sticking out from under the sink, so bent down, carefully unzipped the jeans and started to give him a blow job. Suddenly there was a bang. It turned out that the husband had given up trying to fix the leak and had called a plumber in. The plumber had been so surprised that he'd sat bolt upright and knocked himself out on the sink. The wife panicked and called an ambulance. Worse was to come for the unlucky plumber – when the paramedics heard what had happened, they laughed so hard that they dropped the stretcher and the plumber with it. The poor plumber was laid up in hospital for weeks after multiple skull fractures and an interesting court case followed.

MAN'S BEST FRIEND?

Who says a dog is man's best friend? A man surprised his wife when he started taking their dog for regular evening walks to the park. He told her how much he enjoyed the fresh air and how it took his mind off any problems he was having at work. She was satisfied with this, especially when she saw how contented he seemed when he returned from these walks. One evening, her husband phoned to ask her to take the dog to the park as he had to work late. The wife set out with the dog, but was quite startled when, on leaving the house, the dog dragged her in the opposite direction – to a house just around the corner. She knocked on the front door and an attractive, scantily-clad young woman opened the door. Before anyone could say anything, the dog rushed in, pulling the wife with him. There, reclining on the couch was her half-naked husband.

MIDNIGHT SNACK

A group of women, out on a Saturday night in Berlin, had a few too many drinks in a variety of bars and clubs and decided to finish off with some food at a snack bar on the way home. One of the women ate a hamburger with lots of mayonnaise and felt ill afterwards. So ill that she fainted and her friends took her to hospital, where a doctor examined her concluding that the problem must have been caused by something she ate. He pumped out her stomach and examined the results. He was surprised to identify the sperm of at least three different men. The woman recovered, denied vigorously that she had had oral sex even once that day, and joined her friends in vowing they would never return to that particular snack bar again.

A LITTLE BIT LATE

A teenager returned home on his birthday after an unpleasant day at school where everyone seemed to be going out of their way to ignore him. Although he wondered if his family and friends might have been setting him up for a surprise, arriving home he was greeted as normal. Then his parents told him they were going out – and they left. Lonely and a little sad, the boy telephoned his girlfriend to see if she could join him, but she declined his invitation, stating that she was busy. Irritated at this cold response – on this day of all days – he called up an ex-girlfriend. She willingly visited, and things soon became steamy, so they moved the action upstairs to his bedroom. Ten minutes later, the phone rang and the boy, now naked, went downstairs to answer it, eagerly followed by his naked ex-girlfriend. The call was from his mother, who said she had forgotten to hang up some washing and asked him if he would do it. He agreed and, taking the girl on his back, went into the laundry room to sort out the washing. As he turned on the light there was a shout of "Surprise!" and he saw both his parents, a collection of his school friends and his girlfriend. His mother, seeing her son and his ex-girlfriend naked, stammered quietly "Here's your present," as she handed him a mobile phone.

TWO-WAY CONFUSION

A gay couple decided to have a weekend break by the seaside. They stayed at a small hotel owned by a middle-aged woman who had recently been widowed. Before long, it became obvious to one of the men (who was not entirely gay) that she was quite interested in him. When his partner suggested going for a walk, he declined the offer, explaining that he was tired. As he expected, his partner went for a walk on his own so the man made his move on the woman. They had very passionate sex for several hours but after that their brief liaison was never repeated and it remained a secret. Indeed, in what he considered a cunning move, the man gave the widow his partner's name pretending it was his own. About three years later, the partner received a letter from a lawyer informing him that the widow had died and that she had left him the hotel and all her savings. Along with the lawyer's letter was another letter, this time from the woman, describing in great detail their "afternoon of unbridled passion" which, she asserted, she would not forget until the day she died.

STUCK ON THE JOB

A man and a woman were giving vent to their firey Italian passions in a Fiat Uno, which they had parked in a lay-by near Florence. Suddenly, the man screamed out in pain. In the confined space of the Uno, which is one of the smallest cars in the world, he had strained his back and as a result, couldn't move. His partner was trapped beneath him. Eventually the woman managed to stretch out her hand and start honking the horn. A passing policeman stopped, but realized there was nothing he could do on his own, so he called out the fire service. The firemen solved the problem, but had to cut the roof off the car to free the couple. After the injured man was taken to hospital, the woman started to cry. The policeman tried to reassure her, telling her that her boyfriend would be fine. But she refused to be comforted: "Boyfriend, nothing! My husband will kill me when he sees what has happened to his car!"

ROUND THE BEND

A man called the plumber after finding that his toilet was blocked. The plumber found that the U-pipe was clogged, and, on opening it, discovered the cause: almost a hundred used condoms. The plumber fixed the problem, cleaned up the mess and, on the way out, told the man that he shouldn't flush condoms down the toilet. Soon after, the man packed his bags and left the house, pausing only to leave a note to his wife in which he explained that he was leaving her for good. He also suggested that she should pass on the plumber's advice to her "idiot boyfriend".

TRAVELLERS CHECKED

Unlike their French or Italian counterparts who would have been rather more worldly-wise, the marketing department of one English travel company managed to annoy a significant section of its customers. To promote a service to Paris, frequent travellers in business class were made a special offer: every fourth trip, their spouses could travel with them to the City of Romance for free. The campaign was a great success. That is until the marketing department phoned the spouses of the customers who had participated in the scheme to ask about the service and about their impressions of the promotion. Many of the unsuspecting women promptly replied "What trip to Paris?"

PLAYBACK

A couple spent a romantic weekend at a hotel in a room that was well-equipped for lovers – it featured a hot spa, a television with access to porno films, as well as a large, canopied bed complete with vibrating mattress. The couple had a fantastic time, indulging in all kinds of sexual experimentation, and they decided that this hotel would be a great place for their honeymoon later that year. So after a wonderful wedding, they drove to the hotel, looking forward to another fun-filled weekend. This time around, they stayed in an even plusher suite with panoramic views across the city, a huge bath and all the other luxuries of their previous room. There was also a VCR and several video tapes with titles such as Oral Extravaganza and Bouncy Beds. After a long soak in the hot tub, they relaxed in the luxurious bed and put on a tape. They were getting very turned on by the films, when suddenly the woman shrieked. There, in full colour, but with a dubbed soundtrack, were the two of them in a series of compromising poses caught during their previous stay in the hotel by a hidden camera.

JOKING APART

A young man decided to be well-prepared for a date and so went into a shop to buy some condoms. A middle-aged man served him and noticing that the young man was a bit nervous, decided to joke with him: "You think you might get some tonight then, eh?" The young man chuckled and answered: "No question about it". That evening, all dressed up and feeling lucky, the young man arrived at his date's house and rang the doorbell. His date opened the door and welcomed him inside, saying she just had to visit the bathroom before they left, and motioning him to sit down on the sofa. As he sat down, he heard the girl say: "Oh, Dad, this is Stewart. We're going out tonight." The young man turned round only to recognize his date's father as the shopkeeper he had shared a joke with earlier in the day.

FELINE SURPRISE

A married couple were invited to a New Year's Eve fancy-dress party. The wife organized costumes for them both, but on the night of the party, she developed a bad migraine. She talked her husband into going, so he put on his devil's costume and went out to celebrate while his wife rested in bed. An hour later, the wife's migraine subsided and she decided to join her husband at the party. She also realized that because he had not seen her costume, she could surprise him. Dressed in her Catwoman outfit, she arrived at the party and saw her husband in his devil's costume. She noticed that he was somewhat enamoured by a Marilyn Monroe lookalike, with whom he appeared to be flirting outrageously. Seeing "Marilyn Monroe" leave her husband's side, the wife decided to test his fidelity first-hand and greeted him, miaowing all the way. After a few dances, the husband took her outside and, keeping their masks on, they made love. Afterwards, the wife rushed home and climbed into bed. When her husband eventually returned, she asked him how the night went. Somewhat drunk, he told her that he hadn't been enjoying the party without her, so had lent his costume to a friend and watched videos all night. He added that his mate had seemed to have a good time though…

JAIL BAIT

Ane night, two policemen were doing their usual patrol of the beachfront when they found a tent pitched in a "no camping" area. The first policeman looked inside the tent, saw a young couple having sex and told them that he would have to arrest them for trespassing. Scared of the consequences, the girl offered to give the officer a blow job. He agreed and she delivered her promise while her boyfriend watched. However, to add insult to injury, the officer then told the girl that he would only let them off the hook if she provided the same personal service to his colleague. Seeing that she had little choice, she agreed and the second policeman eagerly entered the tent only to be horrified when he recognized the girl as his 15-year-old daughter.

CLERICAL SURPRISE

One Sunday, after the morning service, a man stayed to help his local priest tidy the church gardens. When they had finished, he invited the priest for dinner and the clergyman accepted. The priest, who was feeling somewhat dirty after the work, asked if he might have a shower before the meal and the man, quite naturally, agreed. His wife, meanwhile, had been cooking dinner and had gone upstairs to tidy herself up. Hearing the shower running and finding the bathroom door unlocked, she assumed that it was her husband using the shower and she entered the room without a second thought. Whilst applying her make-up, she fantasized aloud about what she planned to do to her husband after dinner, describing in detail how his cross-dressing turned her on and how excited she was about the bondage gear they had just bought. Fully made up, she reached through the shower curtain to give the bather's penis a friendly pat before going back downstairs. The wife was startled when she spotted her husband in an armchair watching television, and fainted when he told her that he was waiting to have dinner – once the priest had finished his shower.

NO HEADACHES

A woman was feeling unwell one day and left work early. When she arrived home, she caught her teenage daughter having sex with her boyfriend on the floor in the front room. After admonishing her daughter the mother lectured her about the use of contraceptives and asked her if her boyfriend used condoms. The daughter, angry at being told off, replied that she had actually been using her mother's contraceptive pills for the last two months. The mother, now worried, said that she hadn't noticed any pills missing. The daughter replied smugly that she had been replacing the pills she took with headache tablets. A week later, the mother discovered that she was pregnant.

I'LL CALL YOU...

Just before a couple were due to go on a one-week holiday to Spain, the boyfriend discovered that his girlfriend had been having an affair. Since he had paid for the holiday in full, it seemed foolish not to go, but he decided to take his sister instead of his soon-to-be-ex-girlfriend. Before leaving, he told his girlfriend in no uncertain terms that he wanted her, and all of her belongings, out of his flat before he returned. Arriving home after the holiday, he was pleasantly surprised to find his flat in one piece and actually remarkably tidy – with no detectable trace of his ex-girlfriend. Looking around the room, he noticed that the phone had been left off the hook. He picked up the handset to hear several men talking about sex, so he hung up. When his telephone bill arrived, it included a 150-hour phone call to a chatline number, and a charge that amounted to several thousand pounds.

BARGAIN HUNTER

A man scouring the Items For Sale section of his local newspaper was amazed to see a brand-new BMW car described as being in perfect condition and on offer for the unbelievably low price of £50. Assuming that this must be a misprint, the man immediately called the number, but the woman who answered confirmed that the price was indeed correct. The man promised that he would be there as soon as he could and asked for the address. At the house, a woman answered the door and showed him the car – he could see no obvious problems. After taking the car for a test-drive it was even clearer that the car was in excellent condition throughout. Very pleased with it, he again asked the woman if the price was really £50. It was. Handing over the money, he acquired the necessary papers and the keys, but decided he couldn't leave without knowing why she was selling it so cheaply. She explained matter-of-factly that her husband had left her for another woman a week ago and had told her to sell his car and belongings and forward the proceeds. The man was about to drive off in his new car, when the woman asked him if he'd be interested in buying her husband's almost-new stereo system for ten pounds...

DIRECT ACTION

During the war in former Yugoslavia, a British soldier based in Sarajevo received a package from home. Instead of a letter, it contained a video with the message "To my dear husband. Hope you and your mates enjoy this. Your loving wife." One evening, with a bit of wrangling, the man finally gained access to a VCR and invited his colleagues along to watch the film. As he and his mates had hoped, it turned out to be an amateur porno film. The star was a young woman who, to the delight of the soldiers, was wearing a British Army combat uniform complete with a balaclava hat that covered her head and face – except, that is, for holes for her eyes, nose and mouth. As the film progressed, the woman removed all her clothing except the balaclava and proceeded to have energetic sex in a wide variety of positions with several young men. As the film neared the end, the woman sat up and finally removed the balaclava. Looking straight into the camera, she demanded: "Will you give me a divorce now, you bastard?" The soldier broke down as he recognized his wife on film.

PRIVATE AFFAIR

A victim of a rape attack was testifying in court against her attacker. The prosecutor asked the woman to describe what the attacker had done to her, but she quite naturally became upset – so the judge suggested that she write her answer down for the jury to read, rather than say it out loud in court. The written statement was handed to the jury and each member read it in turn. When one of the jurors, a pretty young woman, finished reading it she nudged the male juror next to her, who had fallen asleep, and passed him the statement. The puzzled juror read it, looked at the woman who passed it to him, turned a bright shade of red and hastily put the note in his shirt pocket. The man looked around and suddenly realized that everybody in the courtroom was staring at him. After a few moments of embarrassed silence, the judge told the man to pass the note to the next juror. The startled man responded: "Please, sir, this is private. You really wouldn't be interested."

CHECKED OUT

A married man from Prague, Czechoslovakia, finally managed to secure a room for a weekend in a holiday cottage after months on a waiting list. Instead of taking his wife, he took his secretary, telling his wife he was going to a conference. The lovers were having an intimate moment when they heard music playing loudly next door. After a while, it began to annoy the man and he told his mistress that he was going to put a stop to it. The woman, anxious that he might get hurt, accompanied him. The man knocked abruptly on the door, and nearly died when his wife opened it. His mistress was equally shocked when she saw her husband, naked, on the bed inside. While the women proceeded to scream at each other, the men ended up fighting until neighbouring holiday-makers came and broke up the altercations. The next morning, the married couples each went their separate ways and as a result of their behaviour were banned from ever using the holiday cottages again.

MAN'S BEST FRIEND

A 60-year-old man lent his video camera to a friend, so that he could film a wedding. A few weeks later, the friend had a showing of the film he made. The newlyweds, their parents and grandparents and various friends including the camera owner, all turned up to watch the film. Everybody seemed delighted with the film and as it drew to an end, they all talked excitedly about what they had seen. All of a sudden the chattering stopped and there was dead silence. The old man, wondering what had happened, looked around to see himself on the television performing sexual acts with his neighbour's dog. Although the man told the jury the footage was an attempt at trick photography, he was found guilty of bestiality and detained in a local psychiatric unit for assessment.

STUCK ON YOU

In a small town in Kenya a liaison between a policeman and one of the wives of a local elder nearly caused a riot. The adulterous couple became stuck together in the middle of the sex act and had no option but to telephone for an ambulance. Somehow, word of their predicament spread and thousands of curious residents began descending on the hospital to get a look at the love-entangled couple. In time, so many people were crammed into the wards and corridors that the hospital security officer called the police for assistance. The police duly arrived and had to use tear gas to disperse the crowds. The humiliated couple were flown to Nairobi where they were eventually separated and given new identities.

BABYFACE?

A not-so-bright couple, who grew up in one of those tiny towns in the American Mid-West, had been married two years. They ran a petrol station on the main highway and business had been surprisingly good, so they decided the woman would stop taking the contraceptive pill and that they would try for a baby. After a year of trying, there was no sign of the baby. The couple were confused. They ate healthy foods and even tried having sex in different positions and at different times of the day. They could not understand why a baby hadn't been conceived, so they decided to see a doctor, the nearest one being in a town 50 miles away. The doctor asked them the relevant questions and examined each of them in turn. On examining the woman, however, he asked her: "How exactly do you have sex?" The woman was too embarrassed to answer, but her husband readily replied: "Oh, you know, doctor, like everyone else… put my ding-a-ling in her mouth and go for it."

BUM QUESTION

A couple had just got married, and the excellent reception was coming to a close. Before the couple were allowed to leave for the honeymoon, mischievous friends of the bride and groom demanded that they take part in a drunken version of the UK TV game show, Mr And Mrs. The wife was led away and made to sit in another room whilst the husband was asked a series of potentially embarrassing questions. The husband felt confident answering the questions until he was asked: "Where was the most embarrassing place you have ever had sex with your new wife?" Red-faced, he eventually answered: "In the toilets about an hour ago." Having caused a few laughs with that, his wife was brought back and made to answer the same questions. The wife was doing very well and every time she gave the same answer that her husband did a little earlier, the friends cheered. When it came to the final question, however, she floundered and looked over at her husband, who said: "Don't worry, honey, I told them." With a pained expression, she whispered: "Up the arse."

SANTA ACTION

A man was about to throw himself off a bridge. His wife had left him, he had lost his job and he owed thousands of pounds to the bank. Just as he finished his prayers and closed his eyes, ready to jump, Father Christmas tapped him on the shoulder: "Are you okay?" The man explained why he was so miserable and got himself ready to jump. "Stop!" shouted Father Christmas. "I will grant you three wishes if you can do me a favour." "Would you?" the man replied, "that would be wonderful. Thank you." Father Christmas granted him his three wishes, and as a result the man decided not to jump – after all, his wife would come back to him and beg for his forgiveness, his boss would beg him to return and give him a £20,000 pay rise, and all his debts would be cleared. "Oh, thank you!" the man said. "What is it that you want me to do for you?" Father Christmas told the man to drop his trousers and bend over. After a somewhat rough sex session, Father Christmas asked the man how old he was. "Thirty-six," replied the man. "You're a bit old to believe in Father Christmas, aren't you?" laughed the jolly, fat homosexual.

FRUSTRATED WIVES

A young English man was talking to a colleague in the pub and explaining how frustrated he was becoming because he couldn't seem to meet any women. His colleague, who was married, told him that he knew just the place and explained that at Seven Oaks, there were dozens of young wives waiting for husbands who were out in the city with their secretaries. The following Friday, the young man took the train to Seven Oaks after work. On arriving at Orpington, however, he noticed lots of pretty women waiting and decided that he might as well try his luck there. He hung around and eventually plucked up the courage to ask an attractive blonde if she would like to go for a drink. He was pleasantly surprised when she said she'd be delighted. They went to a pub and were getting on famously, when the woman exclaimed; "Oh, no, it's my husband!" The woman's husband stormed up to their table and said to his wife: "How could you? After all we've been through!" and then turned to the young man. "As for you - I said Seven Oaks, not Orpington!"

BADLY-TIMED JOKE

A skydiving fanatic introduced his girlfriend to his hobby and she took to it immediately. She loved both the adrenaline rush and the fact that they were sharing the experience. Soon, they were both going skydiving every weekend. One weekend the man decided to propose to his girlfriend on a jump. So, once their parachutes had opened and they were sailing towards the ground, he took a ring from his pocket and asked her to marry him. His girlfriend replied: "Sorry, love, I couldn't. I'm sleeping with your brother." Before she could say anything more, the man snapped off his parachute and yelled at her: "Then let this be on your conscience, you cheating bitch!" and plummeted to his death. The girlfriend was shattered, especially as she was only joking and actually really loved the man.

MANLY AFFAIR

A man met a woman and although she was taller and more heavily-built than him, he fell completely in love. A few days after they first me he asked her to marry him and was overjoyed when she agreed. The next day, they went to Las Vegas, visited a wedding chapel, made their vows and booked into a hotel for their honeymoon. The man was somewhat disappointed, however, when his new wife emerged from the bathroom, wearing a chunky pair of pyjamas, promptly got into bed, turned out the light and gruffly said goodnight. The couple returned to the man's home the next day, but night after night he was let down by his beloved. After a few days of this, the exasperated man tried begging his wife to sleep with him, but to no avail. Days went by and the man became more and more desperate, until one night his wife couldn't take any more of his whining and shouted at him: "Look, you stupid idiot, I'm a bloody man, okay?"

EXPLOSIVE ENDING

A priest from Hungary, sickened that the fall of the Berlin Wall had led not to enlightenment but to sins of the flesh, decided to made a point at his next Sunday service. He brought a variety of sex toys to the church and explained to his startled congregation the uses of each before burning it in a bin. After he showed the congregation a condom, a dildo (with batteries), some sexy lingerie and a porn video, he threw them into the bin, poured petrol over them and set them alight. Thinking that the sermon was over, people began to leave, but the priest barked: "I'm not finished yet. This last item is totally contemptible in the eyes of the Lord!" He pulled out a rubber doll and blew it up to its full size. The congregation stared in disbelief as their priest espoused the doll's despicable and sinful nature. The priest stuffed the rubber doll into the burning bin where it exploded, throwing up pieces of hot latex all over the church and the astonished congregation.

GUILTY CONSCIENCE

A teenage Spanish criminal on the run was browsing in a bookshop when he came across a section in the back full of X-rated porn videos. Feeling mischievous, he bought a video with a title that, roughly translated, means "Three Women Do It". Walking home, excited by the thought of watching the video, the boy spotted a police car parked near his house. Panicking, the boy fled in the opposite direction and hid in an abandoned mill. After a few days, the boy, fed up of eating pieces of stale grain, couldn't take any more, went to the nearest police station and gave himself up, proffering the video for the police sergeant's inspection. The sergeant laughed and said: "But, son, buying porn videos is not illegal. I cannot arrest you for this." The boy couldn't believe his ears and, on finding out that the police had parked outside his house because of a burglary nearby, he ran home to play the video. His relief turned to utter disappointment however, when the video turned out to be about three 40-year-old women talking about leaving their respective husbands to become nuns.

ROMANTIC ENDING

An English woman on holiday in Ibiza met the man of her dreams in a happening nightclub. He was handsome, charming, funny and fantastic in bed. When it came to the end of her holiday and a blissful week with her dream man, the woman reluctantly made her way to the airport. She was delighted when the man caught her just before she was about to went through the passport control. The man gave her a gift-wrapped box and told her not to open it until she was on the plane and that it was something to remember him by. With tears in her eyes, the woman took her seat on the plane and immediately opened her present. Inside, was a big box of condoms and a scribbled note that simply read, “Welcome to the world of AIDS”.

TRAVEL BONDS

A banker and a salesman had been commuting to work together for years and had formed as strong a bond as you can get in such a situation. One day, the salesman boarded the train looking like he was on the verge of tears. With some gentle probing, he revealed that his wife had left him. Eager to cheer him up, the banker invited him for dinner that evening. That night, joining the banker and his wife and daughter for dinner, the salesman began to cheer up and became a frequent visitor to the household. A few weeks later, the banker came across a letter in his daughter's bag. The letter proposed a passionate liaison with the salesman. Furious, the banker told his daughter that he would not permit her to see the salesman but the daughter told him where to go and stormed off in defiance. A week later, the banker confronted the salesman. He said: "Look, you must stop seeing her. It's driving us all apart." To which the salesman coldly replied: "Stop seeing who? Your daughter or your wife?"

HOT DATE

A forty-year-old Casanova-type, complete with orange tan, hairy chest and huge medallion won the attention of an innocent young woman and they arranged to meet at a trendy bar in town that night. The man was walking towards the bar when he passed a department store. Realizing he'd forgotten to put on any scent, he went in and doused himself with lots of free samples. Satisfied, he continued on to the bar and, making sure his hair was greased back and his shirt wide open, he entered the room. To emphasize his macho guise, he popped a cigarette in his mouth and in one swift movement, he took out his Zippo lighter and lit the cigarette, but before he knew it, the flame had reacted with the heavy dousing of perfume and he suddenly burst into flames. The man quickly picked up a pitcher of water and threw it over himself to douse the fire. His new wet look didn't go down very well with his date: she made her excuses and left.

COMING UP FOR AIR

In Auckland, New Zealand, police were initially stumped when they discovered a body of a man in a reservoir. Detectives worked out that the man had used a rope to tie a heavy rock to his ankle and keep him down, but they were mystified to find a pair of scissors with his fingerprints on them at the bottom of the reservoir. However, a week later, a detective received an anonymous message explaining the death. It seems that the man was experimenting with the sexual thrill of self-asphyxiation. The man had tied the rock to his ankle, so that it would hold him beneath the surface. At the last moment, the man had intended to cut the rope, but in his excitement, he had dropped the scissors and drowned.

MEAT AND TWO VEG

A Frenchman was on a business trip in Amsterdam, when he decided to spend an evening off looking around the red-light district. The man cruised around the area for a while, enjoying the window displays, until he spotted a tall, slim, blonde beauty and decided he could not resist her charms. Signalling to the woman, he entered her building through the door at the side where an older woman greeted him before guiding him to a room with a bed in it. The man was relieved when the older woman told him that the blonde woman would be right with him, but explained that it would be better to sort the money out now – so the man paid her before making himself comfortable on the bed. Eventually, the blonde woman entered, began caressing her customer before stripping him and then undressed herself. She was fondling him when the man suddenly cried out, grabbed his clothes and ran. He had noticed that he was about to make love to a hermaphrodite.

PEEK-A-BOOK

A man was plastering the wall of his lounge when he inadvertently made a hole in the wall. Possibly because he hadn't had sex in over a year, the man decided to use the hole for wholly self-gratifying ends. Smearing the edges with grease, he was just reaching climax when a deep thrust caused him to burst through the wall. On the other side, an octogenarian grandmother was engrossed in Coronation Street when she spotted what looked like a snake on the wallpaper. The DIY man ended up in hospital after the grandmother smashed his manhood with a bible in a bid to squash a dangerous snake.

VOYEURIST VEGGIE

In Warsaw, Poland, a banker was disgruntled at the price of watermelon in his local supermarket that he decided to stage a formal protest. When the supermarket was particularly busy, the banker took the manager at gunpoint and ordered him to have sex with each and every watermelon in turn. Customers watched in shock as the manager complied. After the manager had penetrated every watermelon, the security guard jumped on the banker and wrestled him to the ground. "What took you so long?" shouted the humiliated manager. The security guard just shrugged and said: "I would've jumped in sooner but you seemed to be enjoying yourself so much."

FAIRY STORY

A student at Stanford University in California was sharing a room and had been suffering headaches and a sore rectum for some while, so he paid a visit to the doctor, who prescribed a hemorrhoid cream. A week later, the student was still suffering the same problems and another visit to the doctor proved useless. One night, the student ran out of toothpaste and looked in his roommate's cupboard to see if his friend had some that he could borrow. On looking through the cupboard, the student was surprised to find a bottle of chloroform and some Vaseline. Later, the student questioned his roommate, who eventually admitted that he was a homosexual and had thought that drugging him was the only way to relieve his sexual frustration. Surprisingly, the student came around to the idea and the two roommates embarked on a long and loving relationship.

CAMPING IT UP

A middle-aged couple was on campervan holiday in New Zealand. They were staying on a campsite in Queenstown when, early one morning, the wife decided to do some shopping while her husband was asleep. The shopping took a little longer than expected and when the wife returned, she heard some strange noises from inside the campervan. Looking through the window, she saw her husband having sex with a young woman. Angry, the wife got into driving seat, started up the campervan and began to drive it at full speed round and round the campsite, accelerating over all the bumps. Eventually she stopped the vehicle, ordered her husband and his partner to get out of the campervan only to tell the battered and bruised duo that she was leaving them. She drove off.

PREVIOUSLY INTRODUCED

A woman from Nice, France, had the misfortune to be playing with a vibrator when it got stuck and had to go to hospital to have it removed. As if that wasn't embarrassing enough, she had promised to go on a blind double-date with a friend of hers the next night and who should her blind date be? Why, the doctor who had to remove the vibrator, of course!

STICK THAT

A wife from Austin, Texas, found out her husband had had several affairs during their 20 years of marriage and she vowed to put a stop to his philandering ways. One night, when her husband came home drunk and passed out on the couch, she took a tube of Superglue and stuck her husband's penis to his leg.

GREEN GRASS OF HOME

In Mill Valley, California, a man found out his girlfriend was seeing someone else. When she told him she was going away for a business conference, he decided to take revenge. He sprinkled alfalfa seeds all over the carpets of her flat and sprayed them with water before packing all his things and moving out. When the girlfriend came back, her carpets were sprouting like a veritable urban jungle.

SHOCKED AND STUNNED

A husband discovered his wife was having an affair with a colleague from work. He realized that in order to get a divorce, he would need evidence of her infidelity and decided the best way was to record the couple in the act. One evening when he knew his wife was out with her colleague, the man broke into the colleague's flat and hid under the bed, armed with a tape recorder. Not long after, he heard the couple enter the flat and lots of breathless activity and frantic removal of clothes before his wife and her lover jumped on the bed. However, the husband was not counting on their love-making to be so vigorous and before he knew it, the bed was slamming into him repeatedly. The poor husband, forced to emerge from under the bed, would have tried to sneak out had he not fainted from the blows to the head, landing right on top of the dynamic couple. The husband got his divorce, but on the grounds of his wife's evidence that he caused her unprecedented mental abuse by not giving her any privacy.

PIANOFORTE

In Austria, a wife, unhappy in her marriage, seduced the plumber who fixed her washing machine. They were having frantic sex in the kitchen when she heard her husband's car pull into the driveway. With little time to spare the woman bundled the plumber into the grand piano in the lounge and pretended to be dusting when her husband entered. The wife did all she could to get her husband out of the room, but he just collapsed on the sofa and demanded a drink. A few drinks later and the wife had still been unable to persuade her husband to leave the room Suddenly, the door bell rang. Several friends had turned up to say hello. The husband was delighted and opened a special bottle of wine just for the occasion. Knowing the husband to be a good piano player, the friends asked him to play and he enthusiastically relented. On opening up the grand piano, the husband was shocked to see the plumber bunched up over the strings. Not wanting to made a scene, however, he told his friends that the strings were broken and he wouldn't be able to play. The plumber was forced to stay hidden in the piano until the last of the guests had left, at which point, the husband dealt with him ruthlessly.

WRIGGLY BEDFELLOW

A couple inherited a water bed from the wife's grandmother. Having never before slept in a water bed, they planned a whole night of food and drink and sexual activities to inaugurate it in their home. They made the water bed up with silk sheets and then proceeded to gorge themselves on the ultimate aphrodisiac foods and drink before eventually taking themselves upstairs, stripping off their clothes as they went. They collapsed on the bed in a frenzied passion and had the most amazing orgasmic time before drifting off to sleep in each other's arms. In the middle of the night, however, the wife woke up suddenly because she felt the bed moving. She turned on the light and woke up her husband and they watched in shock as the bed writhed and moved as if it had a will of its own. It turned out that water beds need to be treated with a special conditioner to prevent worms growing in the water. The grandmother, who had become senile, had forgotten to treat the water in her final years and, consequently, a huge worm had grown inside. After that fateful night, the couple threw out the water bed and slept on a futon instead.